Bond
No.1 for exam success

Verbal Reasoning

Assessment Practice

Book 1

Ages 9–10   Year 5

Frances Down

OXFORD
UNIVERSITY PRESS

OXFORD
UNIVERSITY PRESS

Great Clarendon Street, Oxford, OX2 6DP, United Kingdom

Oxford University Press is a department of the University of Oxford.
It furthers the University's objective of excellence in research, scholarship,
and education by publishing worldwide. Oxford is a registered trade mark
of Oxford University Press in the UK and in certain other countries

British Library Cataloguing in Publication Data
Data available

978-1-382-05400-3

10 9 8 7 6 5 4 3 2 1

Printed in the UK

The manufacturing process conforms to the environmental
regulations of the country of origin

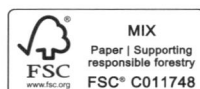

Acknowledgements

Content Development Adviser: Michellejoy Hughes
Page make-up: QBS
Cover illustrations: Lo Cole

Although we have made every effort to trace and contact
all copyright holders before publication this has not been
possible in all cases. If notified, the publisher will rectify
any errors or omissions at the earliest opportunity.

Contents

Welcome

The 11+ exam is used by grammar schools and selective independent schools for entrance into Year 7. It assesses a child in verbal, non-verbal, English and mathematical reasoning, although individual schools may not test all four subjects, and they may combine some of the subjects together. The 11+ covers English and maths topics that a child will be familiar with from the National Curriculum, but supplements these with verbal reasoning and non-verbal reasoning questions.

Bond offers a complete, flexible programme of preparation materials that you can adapt to your child's specific needs and to the requirements of the exam, or exams.

Do remember to keep checking in with your school of choice so that you know which exam they are using. Schools change their exam boards from time to time. When sitting the actual test, there may be an additional time allowance for candidates needing additional support or an exam in a different format, so do also check with your prospective school if your child needs this. Every child has the right to access the 11+ exam and schools will do all that they can to support you.

Is this Book for a Specific Exam Board?

Unless signalled on the front cover as being geared towards a specific exam board, all Bond Verbal Reasoning 11+ materials are designed to hone the flexibility of approach essential to overcoming the challenges of any 11+ exam. The Bond system provides learning, information and consolidation so that children have an extended, rich education.

As different exam boards and schools may have different question types, the 11+ can be challenging to prepare for. This book can be used as preparation for all exam boards as it provides a wide selection of question types and an enriched education is the best preparation. Our aim is to familiarise children with the type of questions they will find in an exam and to give them the transferable skills that will allow a child to attempt any question in any exam. We help children to both master the techniques and develop the logic and rationale to tackle any unknown question types.

This all means that if your child has been working towards an exam from a specific exam board and then the board used by your chosen school changes, all is not lost. This book is good preparation for whichever exam board is being used and the skills covered can be applied to any 11+ exam or independent school entrance exam. It is equally useful for pupils just looking for an extra challenge or wishing to prepare for secondary school.

A Note on Question Formats

The majority of 11+ exams now use a multiple-choice answer format (where your child chooses their answer from a list of options), either entirely or for most of their questions. In Bond practice materials, your child will encounter both multiple-choice questions and some in 'standard format', which is where they have to write or type the answer into a box. We continue to use both because, whilst on the one hand it is good to practise in the format faced in the exam, standard format questions are proven to be more effective for learning and practice. When a child has to decide on an answer themselves without being given options, the simple act of writing out their answer makes their brain work a bit harder and helps those important skills to get stuck in their memory, ready to be used when they sit down for the real test itself.

How Else Can My Child Prepare for the 11+ Exam?

Bond has a wide range of books and resources to support learning. These include flashcards, the *10 Minute Test* books and the *Puzzle* series. Bond Online provides a fun way for your child to consolidate their learning and we offer subscriptions which harness adaptive technology, perfect for building confidence.

KEY STUDY SKILLS

Working towards an entrance exam can be an exciting challenge. It is the chance to learn new things and to prepare for secondary school. Here are some tips to help your child:

- Create a study schedule so that your child has a regular routine.

- Balance short bursts of practice with longer assessment papers.

- Create a quiet study space with pencils, an eraser, paper for working out, books and a notebook for writing down techniques. If they study in different places, keep everything in a box that they can take with them.

- Encourage your child to write down strategies to solve new topics.

- Limit distractions such as television, technology and games when they are studying.

- Remind your child that errors are useful. They are part of the journey to success.

A Note for Parents

Parents have a crucial role in helping children and motivating them. Here are some ways that you can really make a difference.

- Check your child is working at the right level. The goal is being able to score 85% on average. It's demotivating if they can't complete questions. It is also important that they work through the system so they are at the right level for the exam at the right time.

- Mark work promptly and go through errors. If papers have not been marked, a child has no idea how they are doing or whether they are repeating the same mistakes.

- Use the *Bond Handbooks* to help your child understand new techniques.

- Limit the range of homework you give your child. The best results are achieved by a system that gradually increases in difficulty. Completing lots of books and papers doesn't guarantee your child's success and often creates stress.

- If your child is struggling with something specific, add additional support in that area. Use *Bond 10 Minute Tests* for consolidation.

- Communication is key. Encourage your child to focus on the positive. No exam is going to ask for 100%, so pushing for that is unrealistic and stressful.

- If your child is constantly struggling, be realistic about whether a selective education is the right choice at this point in time. Many children move to a selective school for their GCSEs or A levels so not going to a selective school now doesn't mean they never will. It is about finding the best school for your child.

How to Use This Book

This book includes many step-by-step techniques for solving different question types. If further support is needed it can be used alongside one or more of the *Bond Handbooks*, which offer insights into the full range of questions that might occur in the exam.

- The first section of the book is made up of Learning Papers that focus on key skills with worked examples, and then lots of questions for consolidation.

- The second section of the book is made up of Mixed Papers so that children continue to consolidate and do not forget what they have learnt.

- The final section includes two full Test Papers, which can be broken down into shorter sections for more focussed practice, or can be used as full mock tests for that all-important exam practice.

- There is an 11+ Study Guide at the back of the book with some useful hints and tips.

- The removable booklet attached to the back cover includes fully worked out answers to explain how an answer has been reached.

Learning Papers

Synonyms

KEY SKILL

A **synonym** is a word that is similar to another word.

Questions about synonyms are sometimes made more complicated if you do not know the meaning of one or more of the words involved in the question. A good vocabulary is a great advantage. Try to read widely and to be inquisitive about new words.

Questions about synonyms can be phrased in different ways. Mostly, two groups of words are given, and two similar words have to be selected, one from each group.

The possibility of more than one potential meaning for a word means synonym questions can prove tricky. Make sure to read the question carefully and study the example so you can see how to reach the answer.

> **TOP TIP!**
> If you don't know the meaning of a word but it is a multiple-choice question, see how many options you can rule out so that you have fewer options to choose from.

WORKED EXAMPLE Selecting One from Each Group

Underline the two words, one from each group, that are closest in meaning.

(race, shop, start)   (finish, begin, end)

Take each of the words in the left bracket and match them against those in the right bracket. With 'race', none of the words are applicable. You can 'finish', 'begin' and 'end' a 'race' but none of the words mean a 'race'. Try the second word 'shop'. None of the right-hand bracket words mean 'shop'. Therefore, your answer has to be 'start'. Underline it and then find the word on the right that means the same. 'Start' is a synonym of 'begin'. This is the answer.

Underline the two words, one from each group, that are closest in meaning.

1 (health, remedy, doctor)   (chemist, right, cure)

2 (disturb, drill, hasty)   (slow, upset, rush)

3 (tell, offer, demand)   (insist, charge, buy)

4 (travel, area, map)   (direction, house, region)

Key skills highlight the topic then offer tips and strategies to succeed. It is important your child reads these carefully so that they understand the techniques needed.

Worked examples offer support so that your child understands what to do and what to look out for. They should read these carefully. Copying the worked example into a notebook might be helpful for revision.

Timed activity for children to consolidate their skills in an appropriate time.

This Bond 11+ Verbal Reasoning Assessment Practice book is useful for all 11+ exams. The Learning Papers cover the following key skills:

- **Maths, sequences, coding and logic** – working out letter and number sequences and coding and decoding words using numbers, letters or symbols. Questions also include letter coded sums, discovering number relationships and making deductions from given information.

- **Word meanings** – the question types in this section test the ability to identify words that are most similar and most opposite. Vocabulary knowledge is tested through a range of questions, including finding words with multiple meanings.

- **Vocabulary** – including antonyms, synonyms, cloze exercises, spellings and words in context.

- **Making words** – tests the ability to understand how words are made by moving, changing, adding or removing letters. It also includes finding hidden words and missing letters as well as using a rule to create new words. Spelling is tested through problems involving anagrams.

- **Sorting words** – identifying groups of words and placing them into categories. Other questions include finding words that do not belong in a group, placing words in alphabetical order and recognising words with letters in common.

The Mixed Papers ensure the key skills are consolidated thoroughly, then the Test Papers give children the opportunity to get used to the exam process as a natural progression of each book. Don't forget that a rounded education is key. Your child should read as much as they can, play word games, do wordsearches and crosswords, listen to audiobooks, create a vocabulary notebook of words that they don't know and include antonyms and synonyms whenever they can – Bond has a set of Vocabulary Flashcards to help make this more fun. If your child is struggling to read a book, try a book of short stories so that they can read a whole story in one sitting. It is a great way to encounter lots of different authors. They could make a list of those they enjoy and then read their other books. To build inference and deduction skills, encourage active participation. This is reading a paragraph or stopping a programme or movie at regular intervals and asking your child to summarise what has happened. Ask them what a character has done and why they might have done that. What do they think will happen next? Now read or watch some more and they can see if they were correct. As they get more information, their initial views might change and they may need to adapt their viewpoint.

Each book is part of the Bond system with books increasing gradually in difficulty. Once your child has completed this book, there is a clear progression in starting the next book age band if your child has an average score of 85% in this book. If they have achieved an average score of 70%–85%, then another book at this same age band will provide further support. If your child has achieved an average score of less than 70%, then moving down an age band will be most useful. Once your child has then developed the skills needed at this lower age band, they can then move up with confidence. It is often better to begin at a lower age band to build confidence as your child learns and develops their 11+ skills.

Learning Papers

Synonyms

KEY SKILL

A **synonym** is a word that is similar to another word.

Questions about synonyms are sometimes made more complicated if you do not know the meaning of one or more of the words involved in the question. A good vocabulary is a great advantage. Try to read widely and to be inquisitive about new words.

Questions about synonyms can be phrased in different ways. Mostly, two groups of words are given, and two similar words have to be selected, one from each group.

The possibility of more than one potential meaning for a word means synonym questions can prove tricky. Make sure to read the question carefully and study the example so you can see how to reach the answer.

> **TOP TIP!**
>
> If you don't know the meaning of a word but it is a multiple-choice question, see how many options you can rule out so that you have fewer options to choose from.

WORKED EXAMPLE Selecting One from Each Group

Underline the two words, one from each group, that are closest in meaning.

(race, shop, <u>start</u>)   (finish, <u>begin</u>, end)

Take each of the words in the left bracket and match them against those in the right bracket. With 'race', none of the words are applicable. You can 'finish', 'begin' and 'end' a 'race' but none of the words mean a 'race'. Try the second word 'shop'. None of the right-hand bracket words mean 'shop'. Therefore, your answer has to be '**start**'. Underline it and then find the word on the right that means the same. 'Start' is a synonym of '**begin**'. This is the answer.

---

20 mins

Underline the two words, one from each group, that are closest in meaning.

1 (health, remedy, doctor)   (chemist, right, cure) | 1 |

2 (disturb, drill, hasty)   (slow, upset, rush) | 1 |

3 (tell, offer, demand)   (insist, charge, buy) | 1 |

4 (travel, area, map)   (direction, house, region) | 1 |

WORKED EXAMPLE Matching the Synonyms

Underline the word in the brackets closest in meaning to the word in capitals.

UNHAPPY   (unkind   death   laughter   <u>sad</u>   friendly)

First identify the meaning of the word in capitals, in this case UNHAPPY. Then read through the words in the brackets to identify a synonym for unhappy. Work from left to right. Think about the meaning of each word until you find the one that is closest in meaning to the word in capitals. Following this logical process, you will see the answer is **sad**.

Synonyms

Underline the word in the brackets closest in meaning to the word in capitals.

5 START   (end   borrow   begin   borrow   prepare)   `1`

6 FEAR   (frozen   fright   wonder   fall   feeling)   `1`

WORKED EXAMPLE Picking Two Synonyms from a List

Underline the two words in each line which are most similar in type or meaning.

<u>dear</u>   pleasant   poor   extravagant   <u>expensive</u>

Think of the meaning of each of the words in turn and match two that mean the same. '**Dear**' has two meanings: it can mean 'loved' and 'cherished', but it can also mean '**expensive**'.

Underline the two words in each line which are most similar in type or meaning.

7 alter   after   sound   fond   change   `1`

8 sit   fidget   stand   wriggle   kick   `1`

9 ready   Wright   hard   simple   difficult   `1`

WORKED EXAMPLE Rhyming Synonyms

Find a word that is similar in meaning to the word in capital letters and that rhymes with the second word.

CABLE   tyre   <u>wire</u>

If you cannot find a suitable word that is similar to the word in capitals, try experimenting with words that rhyme with the second word. The spelling may be different but the sound of the word will be similar.

Find a word that is similar in meaning to the word in capital letters and that rhymes with the second word.

10 GROUP   stand 1

11 UNEVEN   cuff 1

12 NOT SOUR   bleat 1

WORKED EXAMPLE Links Between Words

Underline the one word in the brackets which will go equally well with both the pairs of words outside the brackets.

rush, attack   cost, fee   (price, hasten, strike, <u>charge</u>, money)

Look carefully at the two groups of words on the left and then study the words in brackets. Take care because more than one meaning will apply to one of the words in the brackets. To 'rush' or 'attack' means to '**charge**', as in run into battle. A 'cost' or 'fee' also means a '**charge**' or the price of something. Sometimes the question isn't looking for exact synonyms, but instead may focus on similar types of word.

Underline the one word in the brackets which will go equally well with both the pairs of words outside the brackets.

13 apartment, rooms   level, even   (flat, home, smooth, habitat, ledge) 1

14 clue, lead   central, important   (hint, lock, key, trail, essential) 1

15 apple, grape   red, yellow   (pear, pineapple, brown, rose, orange) 1

16 price, debt   beak, snout   (invoice, leaflet, nose, paw, bill) 1

17 stone, boulder   sway, move   (cliff, hill, swing, step, rock) 1

WORKED EXAMPLE Relationships Between Words

Underline the word in the brackets that goes best with the words given outside the brackets.

word, paragraph, sentence   (pen, cap, <u>letter</u>, top, stop)

'Word', 'paragraph' and 'sentence' are all connected to writing. 'Letter' goes best with them as letters go to make up words, sentences and paragraphs.

Underline the word in the brackets that goes best with the words given outside the brackets.

18 sleet, snow, rain	(sunny, hot, frost, cool, hail)	1
19 sty, lair, hutch	(flat, bungalow, hotel, cottage, stable)	1
20 sprouts, beans, swede	(oranges, plums, blackberries, carrots, limes)	1
21 talk, chatter, utter	(cough, speak, blow, splutter, sneeze)	1
22 children, teenagers, infants	(age, school, toddlers, adults, grannies)	1

Synonyms

WORKED EXAMPLE Spelling Synonyms

Work out the missing synonym.
Spell the new word correctly, putting one letter in each space.

strange   p e <u>c u l i a</u> r

Start by thinking of words that are similar to 'strange'. Then look at the letters you have been given, thinking of consonant blends and the need for vowels.

Work out the missing synonym. Spell the new word correctly, putting one letter in each space.

23 hard	__ i f f __ c u l t	1
24 rough	c o __ r s __	1
25 comfortable	r e l __ __ e d	1

Total 25

Antonyms

An **antonym** is a word that has the opposite meaning to another word. Just as with synonym questions, a good vocabulary is key. Use a thesaurus and dictionary to help with these practice questions. You will come across other words when you do this, which will help broaden your vocabulary.

Questions about antonyms can be phrased in similar ways to questions about synonyms. So, you need to read the question carefully. Sometimes, it is helpful to consider the answer options before you tackle the question to see how many options you can reject so that you have fewer options to guess from. Be on the look out for the inclusion of synonyms among possible answers.

WORKED EXAMPLE Selecting One from Each Group

Underline the two words, one from each group, that are opposite in meaning.

(down, <u>early</u>, wake)   (<u>late</u>, stop, sunrise)

Take each of the words in the left-hand brackets and match them against those in the right-hand brackets. With 'down', the opposite word would be 'up' but none of the words in the right-hand brackets mean 'up'. The opposite of 'early' is 'late'. The opposite of 'wake' is 'sleep', which does not appear. Therefore, your answer has to be 'early' and 'late'.

20 mins

Underline the two words, one from each group, that are opposite in meaning.

1   (sell, make, use)   (study, purchase, remove)   1 ☐

2   (dim, weak, sturdy)   (bright, mild, blurry)   1 ☐

3   (lesson, question, talk)   (report, teacher, answer)   1 ☐

4   (accept, advance, aware)   (refuse, alive, rubbish)   1 ☐

WORKED EXAMPLE Matching the Antonyms

Underline the word in the brackets which is the most opposite in meaning to the word in capitals.

WIDE   (broad   most   vague   long   <u>narrow</u>   motorway)

Match each of the words in the brackets, in turn, against 'WIDE' to pick out the antonym. In this case, beware of 'broad' which is a synonym. 'Narrow' is the opposite of 'broad'.

Underline the word in the brackets which is the most opposite in meaning to the word in capitals.

5	QUIT	(leave	start	finish	consider	wait)	1
6	PANIC	(calm	precise	worry	bustling	wet)	1
7	HINDER	(prevent	hurt	bother	help	soft)	1
8	LAST	(eternity	finish	halt	endure	first)	1

WORKED EXAMPLE Rhyming Antonyms

Find a word that is opposite in meaning to the word in capital letters and that rhymes with the second word.

SHARP   front   BLUNT

If you cannot find a suitable word that means the opposite of the word in capitals, try experimenting with words that rhyme with the second word. The spelling may be different but the sound of the word will be similar.

Find a word that is opposite in meaning to the word in capital letters and that rhymes with the second word.

9	EXPENSIVE	creep	1
10	WHOLE	heart	1
11	SUCCEED	male	1
12	EAST	crest	1

WORKED EXAMPLE Pairs of Antonyms

Underline the pair of words most opposite in meaning.

cup, mug coffee, milk hot, cold

'Cup' and 'mug' are both drinking vessels. 'Coffee' and 'milk' are both drinks but they cannot be said to be opposite to each other. 'Hot' and 'cold' both refer to temperature and are opposites.

Underline the pair of words most opposite in meaning.

13	circle, round	shiny, dull	enemy, foe	1
14	pause, rest	generous, mean	angry, cross	1
15	home, away	bridge, river	yours, his	1
16	often, seldom	great, big	speak, talk	1
17	tug, pull	raise, lower	push, shove	1

WORKED EXAMPLE Different Groupings

Look at these groups.

M — Money   G — Gardening Tools   C — Carpentry Tools

Choose the correct group for each of the words below. Write the letter.

wheelbarrow **G**   pound **M**   dime **M**   chisel **C**

Start by thinking about what you would use each item for.

18–20 Look at these groups.

M — Money   G — Gardening Tools   C — Carpentry Tools

Choose the correct group for each of the words below. Write the letter.

hammer ___   fork ___   spade ___   dollar ___   trowel ___   cent ___   **3**

WORKED EXAMPLE Odd Ones Out

Underline the two words which are the odd ones out in the following groups of words.

black   <u>king</u>   purple   green   <u>house</u>

Look for the link between three of the words. Here, there are three colours so the other words, '<u>king</u>' and '<u>house</u>', are the odd ones out.

Underline the two words which are the odd ones out in the following groups of words.

21	house	road	bungalow	castle	path	**1**
22	swim	coat	sweater	dive	t-shirt	**1**
23	kneel	sit	walk	hop	skip	**1**
24	butter	cake	bread	bun	flour	**1**
25	onion	apple	plum	cabbage	potato	**1**

Total 25

Finding Words and Letters

KEY SKILL

These types of questions test your spelling skills as well as your vocabulary knowledge and can be presented in different ways. Using the context of the sentence or words can help when you are searching for a word; for an individual letter, running mentally through the alphabet can assist you. Think about the use of vowels and consonant blends when searching for a letter.

WORKED EXAMPLE Finding a Hidden Word

Find the four-letter word hidden at the end of one word and the beginning of the next word in each sentence. The order of the letters may not be changed.

The children had bat<u>s and</u> balls.   *sand*

Start with the first two words. Can you make a four-letter word? the-c? he-ch? e-chi? No. Do the same with all the other words. In this case, it is *s-and*.

To speed the process it might be worth going straight to 'and', because of the vowel at the beginning of the word. It is always worth checking words that begin or end with vowels first as they often contain the answer.

TOP TIP!

If you break the sentence down into two-word sections, you can make sure that you check every gap between the words. Sound out the letters you read.

⏱ 20 mins

Find the four-letter word hidden at the end of one word and the beginning of the next word in each sentence. The order of the letters may not be changed.

1   This book can be very useful.   . . . . |1|

2   There are fairies at the bottom of the garden.   . . . . |1|

3   This house is often cold.   . . . . |1|

4   Will the journey end soon?   . . . . |1|

Finding Words and Letters

WORKED EXAMPLES Finding Letters

Find the letter which will end the first word and start the second word.

peac (**h**) ome

Study each incomplete word and see if anything jumps out to you.
In this example, only an 'e' or 'h' will go on the end of 'peac' to make
a word; 'e' does not work with 'ome' so the answer is '**h**'.

Sometimes you will be asked to find a letter to complete two sets
of words. The same letter has to be used for both sets of words.
Work in the same way, working through the alphabet, adding each
letter to each word in turn. Ask yourself, 'is it a proper word?' 'is it
spelt correctly?'

Find the letter which will complete both pairs of words, ending the first word and starting
the second. The same letter must be used for both pairs of words.

mea (**t**) able   fi (**t**) ub

Find the letter which will end the first word and start the second word.

5   mad (__) rror   `1` ☐

6   ris (__) ing   `1` ☐

7   lis (__) hen   `1` ☐

8   foo (__) rade   `1` ☐

Find the letter which will complete both pairs of words, ending the first word and starting
the second. The same letter must be used for both pairs of words.

9   cuf (__) ringe   mysel (__) ruit   `1` ☐

10   willo (__) and   sno (__) est   `1` ☐

WORKED EXAMPLE Finding a Common Letter

Which one letter can be added to the front of all of these words to make new words?

<u>c</u>are   <u>c</u>at   <u>c</u>rate   <u>c</u>art   <u>c</u>one

Many of these groups of letters can be preceded by another letter, for example, bare, care,
dare, fare, hare, mare, pare, rare, tare, ware. Try and pick a slightly more unusual grouping
of letters like -rate. The answers here could be crate, grate, orate, prate. This immediately
cuts the alternatives down to 'c', 'g', 'o' and 'p'. Now experiment with the options: 'o' does
not work with any of the other words; 'g' does not work with -at or -art; and 'p' does not
work with -one. So the answer must be '<u>c</u>'.

Which one letter can be added to the front of all of these words to make new words?

11 __ row   __ lack   __ east   __ rake   __ at   **1**

12 __ lush   __ east   __ ear   __ lung   __ earful   **1**

WORKED EXAMPLE   Finding a Common Word

Find a word that can be put in front of each of the following words to make new words.

cast   fall   ward   pour   *down*

Look at each of the words in turn and think of words that can go in front of them, for example, waterfall. Then check your word against the other words. In this case, 'water' does not work with the others. Consider 'pour' as it is quite unusual to put a word in front of it. It is always worth considering prepositions and, in this instance, the answer is '*down*'.

TOP TIP!

In this question type, answer words are often colours, or prepositions like up, down, by, under, over, etc.

Find a word that can be put in front of each of the following words to make new words.

13 noon   care   taste   thought **1**

14 bike   car   way   boat **1**

WORKED EXAMPLE   Mixed-up Words

Rearrange the muddled letters in capitals to make a proper word. The answer will complete the sentence sensibly.

A BEZAR is an animal with stripes.   *ZEBRA*

Look carefully at the letters and the sense of the sentence to help you get the right answer. Make sure you spell the word correctly.

Rearrange the muddled letters in capitals to make a proper word. The answer will complete the sentence sensibly.

15 Please don't walk on the AGRSS. **1**

16 Be careful when you cut with a EIKFN. **1**

WORKED EXAMPLE Completing a Word with Another Word

Find the three-letter word which can be added to the letters in capitals to make a new word. The new word will complete the sentence sensibly.

The cat sprang onto the MO.   USE

Complete the sentence sensibly first. What is a cat likely to pounce on? A mouse. The letters you have added onto MO are the answer. Check you have made a proper word.

Find the three-letter word which can be added to the letters in capitals to make a new word. The new word will complete the sentence sensibly.

17 Our dining table has six CHS .... around it.   1

18 The hungry ERPILLAR .... ate a leaf.   1

WORKED EXAMPLE Adding a Letter to Make a New Word

Add one letter to the word in capital letters to make a new word. The meaning of the new word is given in the clue.

PLAN   simple   plain

First look at the clue and think of words that are similar to 'simple', looking at 'PLAN' at the same time. If no luck, think of letters that can inserted into 'plan' to make words and check against the meaning.

Add one letter to the word in capital letters to make a new word. The meaning of the new word is given in the clue.

19 FIGHT   scare   1

20 CRAM   rich milk   1

WORKED EXAMPLE Removing a Letter to Make a New Word

Remove one letter from the word in capital letters to leave a new word. The meaning of the new word is given in the clue.

AUNT   an insect   ant

First look at the clue and think of words that are similar to 'an insect'. In this case, there are many possible alternatives so go quickly on to looking at 'AUNT' and work out which letters can be removed to reach the answer. Here, 'U' is the only letter that can be removed, leaving 'ant'.

Remove one letter from the word in capital letters to leave a new word. The meaning of the new word is given in the clue.

21 SPIRE   father   1

22 TABLE   story   1

Superfluous Word in a Sentence

Superfluous means extra or unneeded. In this case, it refers to an extra word you have to identify.

WORKED EXAMPLE

Rearrange these words into a sentence that makes sense. Underline the word that you do not need.

walk   school   my   minutes   <u>hour</u>   ten   takes   to

(My walk to school takes ten minutes.)

Try and group words together and look for the subject of the sentence, if you can. Here, 'ten minutes' seems to go well together and a possible sentence starter could be 'my'. What could it go with? 'Walk'? 'Hour'? 'School'? Try and locate a verb and something it refers to. By experimenting, you can reach 'takes ten minutes' and go on to complete the sentence, working out that 'hour' is superfluous.

> **TOP TIP!**
> Write out the complete sentence on rough paper, crossing out the words in the question as you go.

Rearrange these words into a sentence that makes sense. Underline the word that you do not need.

23 fluttered   breeze   in   the   the   clouds   kite   colourful

. . . .   1

24 red   has   I   a   may   balloon   please   have

. . . .   1

25 postman   letter   our   gate   the   slams   always   shut

. . . .   1

Total 25

Finding Words and Letters

19

Sorting Words and Letters

KEY SKILL

This section involves manipulating different words, thinking about the order of letters and rearranging words. Read carefully, think of letter combinations and the position of vowels, and use the sense of the sentence when you can.

WORKED EXAMPLE Choosing a Word to Make a Sentence Logical

Find and underline the word or phrase that makes each sentence true.

A LIBRARY always has (posters, a carpet, <u>books</u>, DVDs, stairs).

Think about what the word in capital letters has to have. Many things in the example above may be found in a library but a library is mainly for books.

> **TOP TIP!**
> Take note of the word 'always'.

---

20 mins

Find and underline the word or phrase that makes each sentence true.

1   A BIRD always has a (nest, beak, chick, worm, twig).   `1`

2   A FOREST always has (flowers, berries, birds, trees, a pot).   `1`

WORKED EXAMPLE Replacing a Word

Change one word so that the sentence makes sense. Underline the word you are taking out and write your new word on the line.

I waited in line to buy a <u>book</u> to see the film.   *ticket*

Work out what the sentence is trying to say. If you are in a queue wanting to see a film, the likelihood is you are waiting to buy a ticket.

> **TOP TIP!**
> Use the sense of the sentence to guide you.

Change one word so that the sentence makes sense. Underline the word you are taking out and write your new word on the line.

3   As it was hot and stuffy, I closed my bedroom window.   ....   `1`

4   After swimming, I dried myself on my raincoat.   ....   `1`

Selecting Anagrams in a List

Anagrams are words that can be made into new words by rearranging the letters.

WORKED EXAMPLE

Underline the two words in each line which are made from the same letters.

TAP   PET   <u>TEA</u>   POT   <u>EAT</u>

Look through each of the words and check for similar letters.

Underline the two words in each line which are made from the same letters.

5 PIANO   PLATE   PLAYS   PEDAL   PETAL   1 ☐

6 SHALL   HOUSE   SHORE   HOMES   HORSE   1 ☐

WORKED EXAMPLE Forming an Anagram

Rearrange the letters in capitals to make another word. The new word has something to do with the first two words.

spot   soil   SAINT   <u>STAIN</u>

Study the word 'SAINT'. Shuffle the letters in your mind while thinking about the clues. If a piece of material is marked with a 'spot', or 'soiled', it can be said to be stained.

TOP TIP!

Use the clues to help you while mentally rearranging the letters of the word in capitals.

Rearrange the letters in capitals to make another word. The new word has something to do with the first two words.

7 start   commence   BEING   . . . .   1 ☐

8 beneath   lower   ELBOW   . . . .   1 ☐

9 inexpensive   economical   PEACH   . . . .   1 ☐

Combining Two Words

New, longer words can be formed by joining two other words together.

WORKED EXAMPLE

Underline two words, one from each group, that go together to form a new word. The word in the first group always comes first.

(hand, <u>green</u>, for)   (light, <u>house</u>, sure)

Match each of the words in the second group with 'hand'. None of them make words. Repeat with 'green'. A greenhouse is where plants may be grown. Check 'for' to be certain, but the answer here is '**greenhouse**'. Underline both words.

Underline two words, one from each group, that go together to form a new word. The word in the first group always comes first.

10 (name, pay, try)   (less, use, more)   **1**

11 (on, be, in)   (head, wind, shoulders)   **1**

12 (chapter, page, text)   (book, mark, word)   **1**

WORKED EXAMPLE Missing Words

Complete the following sentences by selecting the most sensible word from each group of words given in the brackets. Underline the words selected.

The (<u>children</u>, books, foxes) carried the (houses, <u>books</u>, steps) home from the (greengrocer, <u>library</u>, factory).

Let the sense of the sentence guide you to the most appropriate answer. In this example, after the first set of brackets, 'carried' leads you to the fact that 'children' and 'foxes' can carry things. 'Books' can't. 'Foxes' are unlikely to carry any of the things in the second brackets. Therefore '**children**' and '**books**' are the most probable answers so far, leading to 'library' as the most likely answer in the third gap.

TOP TIP!

Read the sentence across the gaps to get the sense of it, then apply the words to each gap.

Complete the following sentences by selecting the most sensible word from each group of words given in the brackets. Underline the words selected.

13 The (farmer, sailor, boy) was going to the (docks, shed, swimming pool) to (shop, milk the cows, read a book).

`1`

14 Ann took her (spoon, spade, hoe) to the (garden, beach, park) as she wanted to build a (bridge, castle, palace).

`1`

15 Don't (put, lose, forget) to (find, eat, post) this (stamp, stock, letter).

`1`

16 The (television, friend, lantern) lit his (face, knee, elbow) as he (ran, threw, buried) the treasure.

`1`

WORKED EXAMPLE Swapping Words

Find and underline the two words which need to change places for each sentence to make sense.

She went to <u>letter</u> the <u>write</u>.

Unscramble the sentence by reading carefully to get the sense. Then locate the words that need to be swapped. Here the position of the verb, 'write', leads you to the correct answer.

> ### TOP TIP!
> **Study the sentence carefully and let your common sense identify the words that need to be switched.**

Find and underline the two words which need to change places for each sentence to make sense.

17 As tights is cold I am wearing it.

`1`

18 I'm sorry glass broken the I've.

`1`

19 I'll home to get him have.

`1`

WORKED EXAMPLE Selecting a Word

Underline the one word which **cannot be made** from the letters of the word in capital letters.

STATIONERY   stone   tyres   ration   <u>nation</u>   noisy

Look at each of the words in turn, starting with 'stone'. All the letters of this word can be found in 'STATIONERY'. Work through the others in the same way. 'Nation' is the answer: all the letters do feature in 'STATIONERY' but 'n' is used twice in 'nation', whereas there is only one 'n' in 'STATIONERY'.

Underline the one word which **cannot be made** from the letters of the word in capital letters.

20 TERRACE   car   rate   trace   erase   crate   [1]

21 DISTANT   stead   stand   stain   ants   dint   [1]

22 PAINTER   trip   rain   tramp   nape   print   [1]

WORKED EXAMPLE

Underline the one word in each group which **can be made** from the letters of the word in capital letters.

CHAMPION   camping   notch   peach   cramp   <u>chimp</u>

This question type can be treated in exactly the same way as the type above, except this time you are looking for a word that *can* be made. Each of the words, apart from 'chimp', has letters that do not appear in 'CHAMPION'.

Underline the one word in each group which **can be made** from the letters of the word in capital letters.

23 GENERAL   large   rages   learnt   grain   gland   [1]

24 DETAINS   nears   nests   instant   staid   seated   [1]

25 CRINGES   crime   rising   rinse   cages   inner   [1]

Total 25

Substitution, Number and Logic

KEY SKILL

This learning paper covers the following types of verbal reasoning questions:

- logic problems
- alphabetical order questions
- letter-coded calculations
- crosswords.

You will need sound mental arithmetic skills, to be able to carry out calculations confidently using addition, subtraction, multiplication and division and to think through questions logically.

Read the questions carefully, use rough paper to assist you and think logically using the information you have been given.

WORKED EXAMPLE Substitution

If A = 6, B = 2, C = 5, D = 12 and E = 3, find the value of the following calculations.

(D ÷ E) + 3C   **19**

To complete this type of question, follow the rules of BIDMAS: complete the brackets first, then the multiplication, then the division and finally the addition and then the subtraction.

Brackets must be completed first. D = 12 and E = 3, therefore 12 ÷ 3 = 4.

Next: C = 5, so 3 × C (5) = 15.

Finally, 4 + 15 = **19**.

> **TOP TIP!**
> A letter next to a number, like 3A, means 3 × A.

⏱ 25 mins

If A = 2, B = 3, D = 4, E = 5, F = 6 and G = 8, find the value of these calculations. Give your answers as a letter.

1 G – B =   ____   1

2 F ÷ A =   ____   1

3 (E + D) – F = ____   1

4 2A =   ____   1

5 A + B =   ____   1

WORKED EXAMPLE Finding Missing Numbers

Find the missing number by using the two numbers outside the brackets in the same way as the other sets of numbers.

2 [8] 4   3 [18] 6   5 [**25**] 5

Solve these questions by looking at the first set of three and working out how the first and last numbers have been used to arrive at the middle number. Apply your answer to the second set of three and see if it works. If it does, apply it to the last set.

Here, 2 × 4 = 8.

Check the same method in the second group: 3 × 6 = 18.

Multiply the last group, 5 × 5 = 25 to reach the answer.

Find the missing number by using the two numbers outside the brackets in the same way as the other sets of numbers.

6   18 [3] 6   20 [5] 4   16 [__] 8

7   2 [18] 9   3 [12] 4   6 [__] 4

8   11 [14] 3   5 [5] 0   8 [__] 7

9   10 [100] 10   4 [16] 4   8 [__] 8

10   13 [2] 11   10 [6] 4   9 [__] 8

WORKED EXAMPLE Logic

A, B, C, D, E and F were asked their favourite colours.

A and B like blue.

C likes green but not red.

F likes red and green.

B dislikes green but E only likes green.

Yellow is liked by the person who dislikes red. D also likes yellow.

Which colour is the most popular?   green

Which colour is the least popular?   red

How many more like blue than red?   1

How many only like one colour?   4

On a piece of rough paper, draw a table or write a list to sort out the information.

	Blue	Green	Red	Yellow
A	✓			
B	✓	✗		
C		✓	✗	✓
D				✓
E		✓		
F		✓	✓	

11–12 Five children did a test for which 100 marks were awarded.

R got 96 marks.

M had half as many marks as the person who was first.

G lost 5 marks.

D had 7 fewer than G.

S had 12 marks fewer than R.

How many marks did these children get?

M _____   G _____   D _____   S _____

WORKED EXAMPLE Logical Statements

Read the first two statements and then underline one of the four options below that must be true.

'Mum's roses are red. Many roses are scented and some have thorns.'

A Mum's roses are thornless.

B Scented roses may be red.

C Scented roses have thorns.

D Roses are scented and may have thorns.

Work out what has to be true according to the information.

The first sentence is giving you specific information about particular roses whereas the second sentence is giving you general information.

Look at the options and compare them with the first two sentences.

A: You cannot know that Mum's roses are thornless for sure.

B: This option is possible. (We know roses can be red, and we know many roses are scented.)

C: This option states all scented roses are thorny. Based on the information you have, you cannot be sure of this.

D: The second sentence states that many roses are scented, but this does not mean all are.

Substitution, Number and Logic

Read the first two statements and then underline one of the four options below that must be true.

13 'Guitars are musical instruments. Guitars have strings.'

   A All musical instruments have strings.

   B All musical instruments need electricity.

   C Guitars are stringed instruments.

   D Strings are musical instruments.

   `1`

14 'People like living in houses. Houses are usually made of brick.'

   A Some people live in flats.

   B Houses are popular.

   C Houses have gardens.

   D All houses are built of brick.

   `1`

WORKED EXAMPLE Alphabetical Order

   douse   double   down   doubt   dough

If these words were placed in alphabetical order:

which word would be last? _down_   which word would be first? _double_

If the words were written backwards, which would be the last in alphabetical order? _doubt_

Arrange the words in a grid to help you:

D	O	U	B	L	E
D	O	U	B	T	
D	O	U	G	H	
D	O	U	S	E	
D	O	W	N		

If these words were placed in alphabetical order:

15 baby   schoolgirl   student   grown-up   pensioner

   Which word would be first? . . . .   `1`

16 seed   seedling   leaf   bud   flower

   Which word would be last? . . . .   `1`

17 pram   pushchair   tricycle   bicycle   car

Which word would be fourth?   1

18 letter   word   sentence   paragraph   book

Which word would be second?   1

19 none   single   triple   quadruple   double

Which word would be third?   1

20 If the letters in the word BANANA were put in
alphabetical order, which would come fourth?   1

WORKED EXAMPLE Crosswords

Fill in the crosswords so that all the given words are included. You have been given one
letter as a clue in each crossword.

risky

seeds

every

taste

taper

piece

Work from the given letter. Place that word which will lead to the others.

Place 'risky' first as you are given the 'k'. From this you can place 'every' and 'taper' and
then the other words.

Fill in the crosswords so that all the given words are included. You have been given one
letter as a clue in each crossword.

21

cared, comic, court, timid, usher   1

22

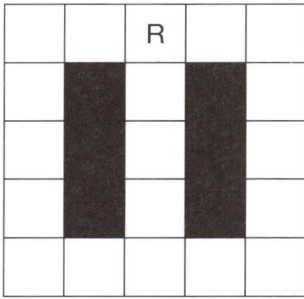

Egypt, early, evade, yacht, ready

1

23

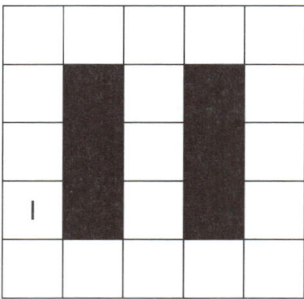

clear, madam, major, delve, music

1

24

pipit, prove, pushy, treat, store

1

25

meals, motor, riper, plant, riser

1

Total
25

30

Word Progressions

KEY SKILL

With these questions, you need to track how the letters are changing and identify the patterns, then complete the questions in the same way.

WORKED EXAMPLE Moving Letters and Making New Words

Move one letter from the first word and add it to the second word to make two new words.

hunt   sip   hut   snip

Work out which letter can be removed from 'hunt' so the remaining letters still make a word. The only one is 'n', to leave 'hut' and turn 'sip' into 'snip'.

TOP TIP!

Sometimes more than one letter can be removed from the first word leaving a possible word behind, so take care that the letter you remove can make a new word when added to the second word.

⏱ 20 mins

Move one letter from the first word and add it to the second word to make two new words.

1	bear	link	....	....	1 ☐
2	clean	breath	....	....	1 ☐
3	land	fake	....	....	1 ☐
4	done	well	....	....	1 ☐
5	splice	sides	....	....	1 ☐

WORKED EXAMPLE Changing Words to Match Pairs

Change the first word of the third pair in the same way as the other pairs to give a new word.

bind, hind   bare, hare   but, hut

Each set of words has been changed in the same way. Study the first two pairs and follow the same method to find the missing word.

The pattern here is to rhyme the second word with the first, changing the first letter from 'b' to 'h'. So 'but' becomes '**hut**'.

Change the first word of the third pair in the same way as the other pairs to give a new word.

6	pack, peck	ball, bell	band, ...		1
7	sing, wing	sink, wink	sail, ...		1
8	mile, lime	sent, nest	love, ...		1
9	peal, pale	bear, bare	deal, ...		1
10	hate, heat	fowl, flow	hire, ...		1

WORKED EXAMPLE Removing Letters to Make a New Word

Remove two letters from the word in capital letters to leave a new word. The meaning of the new word is given in the clue.

MONKEY   lives in a monastery   **monk**

Look for your new word, using the clue to help you.

Experiment with letters you can remove, leaving a word behind, and then check against the meaning in the clue. Here, if you remove 'M', a word beginning 'O' is not looking promising. Taking away the 'K' makes the word 'MONEY' but you cannot remove another letter successfully. However, removing the last two letters 'EY' leaves '**monk**' which matches the clue.

Remove two letters from the word in capital letters to leave a new word. The meaning of the new word is given in the clue.

11	STREET	a tall plant	. . . .		1
12	LEARNT	tilt	. . . .		1
13	STRAND	on a beach	. . . .		1
14	FRAMES	celebrity	. . . .		1
15	SPRAIN	twirl	. . . .		1

WORKED EXAMPLE Using Given Letters to Make a New Word

Look at the first group of three words. The word in the middle has been made from the other two words. Complete the second group of three words in the same way, making a new word in the middle.

PAIN   INTO   TOOK   ALSO   SOON   ONLY

Use a grid to help you work out the missing word.

Look at the first group of three words.

The first two letters of 'INTO' come from the last two letters of 'PAIN', so mark letter I as 1 and letter N as 2.

The third and fourth letters of 'INTO' come from the first three letters of 'TOOK'. (The 'O' could come from the second or the third letter of 'TOOK'.) Mark letter T as 3, and mark both of the Os as 4.

Then transfer the numbers to the second group of words. The last two letters of 'ALSO' give you 'SO'. The first letter of 'ONLY' gives you 'O' and the second and third give you either 'N' or 'L'. 'N' fits onto 'SOO' to make 'SOON'.

		1	2		3	4?	4?						1	2		3	4?	4?	
P	A	I	N		T	O	O	K			A	L	S	O		O	N	L	Y

Word Progressions

TOP TIP!

Take care when the same letter could be taken from more than one place.
Adding a question mark to the options in the grid is a good idea.

Look at the first group of three words. The word in the middle has been made from the other two words. Complete the second group of three words in the same way, making a new word in the middle.

16 HERB   BARK   ASKS   AJAR   ....   EELS

17 CITY   TYPE   PEAS   BONE   ....   STIR

18 MAIL   WAIT   THAW   SOUR   ....   LEAF

19 ENDS   DICE   ICON   SOBS   ....   EDGE

20 TINS   BIND   DRAB   WOOD   ....   KILT

WORKED EXAMPLE Making a New Word by Changing Letters

Change the first word into the last word by changing one letter at a time and making a new, different word in the middle.

CASE   CASH   LASH

Identify the letters that stay the same and write them down. Then look at the letters that need to change.

'A' and 'S' stay the same. The 'C' needs to become 'L' and the 'E' needs to become 'H'. Experiment making a word by changing these letters; for example, 'LASE' isn't a word whereas 'CASH' is. The 'C' can then be changed to 'L' to make 'LASH'.

Change the first word into the last word by changing one letter at a time and making a new, different word in the middle.

21 SEND   ....   SANG   1

22 CAKE   ....   MALE   1

23 DEAR   ....   MEAL   1

24 CALL   ....   BAIL   1

25 HOME   ....   COMB   1

Total
25

Codes

WORKED EXAMPLE Simple Letter Codes

If the code for **MATERIAL** is a h c b x q h v, what is the code for **REALM**?   x b h v a

Match the code letters to the letters of the word.
R = x, E = b, A = h, L = v, M = a

If the code for **STEAM** is a b c d e, what are the codes for the following words?

1 MAST   ....   `1`

2 TAME   ....   `1`

What do these codes stand for?

3 e c a a   ....   `1`

4 e d b c   ....   `1`

WORKED EXAMPLE Simple Number Codes

If the code for **SIMPLIFY** is 73529364, decode 73994.   SILLY

Match the numbers to the letters. 7 = S, 3 = I, 9 = L, 9 = L, 4 = Y.

If the code for **PLANTER** is 8 3 6 4 7 5 2,

5 what is the code for **ANTLER**?   ....   `1`

Using the same code, decode the following:

6 8 3 6 4 5   ....   `1`

7 8 3 5 6 7   ....   `1`

WORKED EXAMPLE Simple Sign Codes

If the code for **P R O T E C T**
is **£ ! : * ? / *** ,

what is **T O R E**?   * : ! ?

Match the numbers to the letters. T = *, O = :, R = !, E = ?.

Using the same code:

8 what is **PORT**? 1

9 what is **CROP**? 1

10 Using the same code, decode **? ! ? / ***. 1

WORKED EXAMPLE Simple Mixed Codes

If the code for **C E N T E N A R Y**
is **P m 4 W m 4 % 8 u** ,

what is the code for **TRACE**?   W 8 % P m

Match carefully. T = W, R = 8, A = %, C = P, E = m.

If the code for **TEACHER** is **% 7 y * z 7 B,** decode these:

11 * z 7 y % 1

12 % B y * 7 1

WORKED EXAMPLES Matching Codes to Words

Here are the codes for four words. Match the right word to the right code.

MAN	AND	MEN	AN
$\frac{1}{2}$ # $\frac{1}{4}$	$\frac{1}{2}$ $\frac{3}{4}$ $\frac{1}{4}$	$\frac{3}{4}$ $\frac{1}{4}$	$\frac{3}{4}$ $\frac{1}{4}$ @

MAN = $\frac{1}{2}$ $\frac{3}{4}$ $\frac{1}{4}$ AND = $\frac{3}{4}$ $\frac{1}{4}$ @   MEN = $\frac{1}{2}$ # $\frac{1}{4}$ AN = $\frac{3}{4}$ $\frac{1}{4}$

Start by looking at the length of the words: some may be able to be matched immediately to the right codes. Then look for common letters and repeats to help match the codes.

The first word and code to match is AN and $\frac{3}{4}$ $\frac{1}{4}$ as this is the only two-letter word and code.

From this, AND must equal $\frac{3}{4} \frac{1}{4}$ @ and also MAN = $\frac{1}{2} \frac{3}{4} \frac{1}{4}$, leaving MEN = $\frac{1}{2}$ # $\frac{1}{4}$.

Match the right code to each of the words below. One of them has been missed out. Then answer the questions below.

CLAM	LAMB	BIKE	LICK
6128	8427	3612	

CLAM   **3612**   LAMB   **6128**

BIKE   **8427**   LICK   **6432**

What is the code for **CAME**?   **3127**   Decode 2462   **MILK**

Look for common letters and repeats to help match the codes. Then identify other letters in the words which can then lead you to solving the codes and working out what the missing code is.

Two words begin with 'L'. However the codes supplied all begin with different letters so the code for either 'LAMB' or 'LICK' must be missing.

Two words have 'LAM' in them. So look for the same three numbers in the same order appearing in two different codes.

Identify 'LAM' as '612'. From this you know CLAM = 3612 and 'LAMB' is '6128'. You can also deduce that '8427' must be 'BIKE' and from the letters you now know, you can work out that 'LICK' = '6432'.

'CAME' = 3127 as C = 3, A = 1, M = 2 and E = 7.

2462 = 'MILK' as M = 2, I = 4, L = 6 and K = 7.

Here are the number codes for four words. Match the right code to the right word.

RINK	KIN	INK	RANK
9 3 5	7 1 5 9	7 3 5 9	3 5 9

13 RINK   ....

14 RANK   ....

15 INK   ....

16 KIN   ....

17 Using the same code, which of these stands for **NEAR**?

    3 6 1 7   5 7 1 7   5 6 1 7   ....

18–25

Here are the number codes for three of the four words. Match the right code to the right word and work out the missing code.

MAST	STAR	REST	TEA
5 3 1 4	4 3 2	7 2 1 4	

18 MAST .... ☐ 1

19 STAR .... ☐ 1

20 REST .... ☐ 1

21 TEA .... ☐ 1

22 Write **REAM** in code. .... ☐ 1

23–25

Match the correct codes to the words and work out the missing one.

MAST	PLAN	LEAP
q m 4 k	m * 4 q	

23 PLEA .... ☐ 1

24 PLAN .... ☐ 1

25 LEAP .... ☐ 1

Total 25

38

Sequences

Sequences follow a pattern. This needs to be identified and then followed.
Work carefully, through using an alphabet line to help you with letter sequences.

A B C D E F G H I J K L M N O P Q R S T U V W X Y Z

WORKED EXAMPLE Word Sequences

Complete the following sentences in the best way by choosing one word from each set of brackets.

Tall is to (tree, short, colour) as narrow is to (thin, white, wide).

Look for the relationship between the pairs of statements. The second pairing must be completed in the same way as the first.

Read the sentence and select words to balance each other. 'Tall' and 'narrow' do not have any relationship, so study the brackets. 'Trees' can be tall but there is nothing to balance 'narrow' in the same way in the second brackets. 'Tall' and 'short' are opposites and 'narrow' and 'wide' are opposites. Check the other options to make sure you have selected the correct answer.

20 mins

Choose two words, one from each set of brackets, to complete the sentences in the best way.

1   Tuesday is to Wednesday as (May, March, April) is to (March, May, July). `1`

2   Puppy is to dog as (cat, lamb, ewe) is to (dog, sheep, pig). `1`

3   Author is to book as (man, sculptor, artist) is to (picture, paint, woman). `1`

4   Plate is to eat as (knife, cup watch) is to (drink, fork, saucer). `1`

5   Aunt is to niece as (mother, uncle, nephew) is to (nephew, boy, sister). `1`

WORKED EXAMPLE Letter Sequences in Sentences

Fill in the missing letters. The alphabet has been written out to help you.

A B C D E F G H I J K L M N O P Q R S T U V W X Y Z

AB is to CD as PQ is to **RS**.

Look at the relationship between the first two pairs of letters. Here it is a simple alphabetical run, 'ABCD', so in the second pairing it will be 'PQRS'. In many questions the letters work independently so look at the first letter of the first pair and work out the relationship with the first letter of the second pair. Then repeat for the second letters in each pair.

Sometimes the letter sequences are based on alphabetical order with letters missed out, or repeated letters. When you meet a new sequence, always check to see if you can spot other patterns at work.

Fill in the missing letters. The alphabet has been written out to help you.

A B C D E F G H I J K L M N O P Q R S T U V W X Y Z

6   AB is to CD as EF is to _____ .   1

7   AC is to DF as GI is to _____ .   1

8   M2 is to N4 as O6 is to _____ .   1

9   9BC is to 12BC as 15BC is to _____ .   1

10 8AB is to 6BC as 4CD is to _____ .   1

WORKED EXAMPLE Letter Sequences

Give the two missing groups of letters in the following sequences. The alphabet has been written out for you.

A B C D E F G H I J K L M N O P Q R S T U V W X Y Z

CQ   DP   EQ   FP   **GQ**   **HP**

Discover the pattern and follow it through the sequence.

Sometimes the letters work independently; other times, they work as a pair.

Here, the letters work independently. The first letters follow alphabetical order, so the first letters in the missing pairs are G and P. The second letters follow a repeating pattern, QPQPQP. So, the missing pairs are GQ and HP.

Give the two missing groups of letters in the following sequences. The alphabet has been written out for you.

A B C D E F G H I J K L M N O P Q R S T U V W X Y Z

11 AH BI AJ BK __AL__ __BM__

12 __BA__ __DC__ FE HG JI LK

13 RC PX __NC__ __LX__ JC HX

14 __GiH__ IkK __KmN__ MoQ OqT QsW

15 JQ KP LO MN __NM__ __OL__

WORKED EXAMPLE Number Sequences

Give the two missing numbers in the following sequences.

2   4   6   8   **10**   **12**

Look at the pattern and continue in the same way. Here, it is simply to add 2 each time.

Give the two missing numbers in the following sequences.

16 91 __82__ 73 64 __55__ 46

17 __$\frac{1}{2}$__ $\frac{3}{4}$ __1__ $1\frac{1}{4}$ $1\frac{1}{2}$ $1\frac{3}{4}$

18 70 __63__ __56__ 49 42 35

19 66 77 88 __99__ __110__ 121

20 1 2 4 7 __11__ __16__

WORKED EXAMPLE Mixed Sequences

If you have letters and numbers together, work through each in turn. Make sure you use capital and lower case letters in the correct places.
Give the two missing letters and numbers in the following sequences.

3Ga   5Jb   7Mc   9Pd   **11Se**   **13Vf**

Take each letter/number in turn.

Start here with the first numbers in each group. Look at the pattern: 3, 5, 7, 9. In this sequence, 2 is added each time. Write the next two numbers in the sequence: 11 and 13.

Next, look at the capital letters. They move forward three alphabetical places each time: G, J, M, P, so write the next two letters in the sequence: S and V.
Lastly, look at the lower case letters. They are in alphabetical order so add the next two, e and f.

Give the two missing numbers in the following sequences.

21 BK66   BL55   CM45   _____   _____   DP15 | 1 |

22 2P   _____   8T   11V   14X   _____ | 1 |

23 _____   Y8B   X7C   _____   V5E   U4F | 1 |

24 TV9   UT6   _____   WP6   _____   DL6 | 1 |

25 DcB   EdD   FeF   _____   _____   IhL | 1 |

Total
25

42

Curveball Questions 1

Another Dimension to Alphabetical Order

Another Dimension to Alphabetical Order

KEY SKILL

Verbal reasoning makes you think about words in a variety of ways, sometimes using words to test your vocabulary, how words are used and manipulating them in different patterns and sequences or finding differences. It is also important to have a good knowledge of the structure of words, sounds, blends and changing letters.

Here, we are going to manipulate words using alphabetical order. Putting a list of words in alphabetical order is taken to a different dimension. The questions are all mixed up, so read carefully.

20 mins

A B C D E F G H I J K L M N O P Q R S T U V W X Y Z

1 If the letters of EXHAUST were arranged in alphabetical order, which letter would come in the middle? .... ☐ 1

2 If these words were placed in alphabetical order, which would come fourth?

human   hound   honey   house   hours   .... ☐ 1

3 Which of these words starts with the nineteenth letter and ends with the twentieth?

SUSPECT   TARGET   TORCHES   SAUCES   .... ☐ 1

4 Rearrange the first, second, fifth, eighteenth and twenty-sixth letter to make a word. .... ☐ 1

5 If the letters of RHYTHM were arranged in alphabetical order, which letter would come fourth? ....

6 Write these words in reverse alphabetical order:

precise   precious   pretty   previous   preen   precipice

.... ☐ 1

43

7 Rearrange the fourteenth, two of the fifteenth letters, the
sixteenth and the nineteenth letters to make a five-letter word . . . . 　1

8 If these words were placed in alphabetical order, which would come fourth?

region　　parade　　patrol　　reason　　reader　　　. . . . . 　1

9 Put the letters in the word QUESTION in alphabetical order.
Which is now the third letter?　　　　　　　　　　. . . . . 　1

10 If the letters of HAMBURGER were arranged in alphabetical
order, which letter would come in the middle?　　　. . . . . 　1

11 Which of these words starts with the eighth letter of the alphabet and finishes
with the fifteenth?

HIPPO　　　　HAMPER　　　　HYPHEN　　　. . . . . 　1

12 Which word in the list contains only the first eight letters of the alphabet?

arrow　　beady　　beach　　creed　　bread　　　. . . . . 　1

If these words were listed in reverse alphabetical order, which word would come second?

13 charade　　chorus　　chamber　　chemist　　chivalry　　. . . . . 　1

14 fraction　　friction　　frostbite　　frown　　friend　　　. . . . . 　1

15 trampoline　　train　　trophy　　treasure　　trellis　　　. . . . . 　1

16 Which word in the list contains only the first eight letters of the alphabet?

finch　　baffle　　dance　　defeat　　hedge　　　. . . . . 　1

17 Rearrange the first, third, fourth, fifth and fourteenth
letters of the alphabet to make a word.　　　　　　. . . . . 　1

18 Write these words in reverse alphabetical order:

cushion　　customary　　culinary　　culture　　cupboard　　curable

. . . . 　　. . . . . 　　. . . . . 　　. . . . . 　　. . . . . 　　. . . . . 　1

19 Which of these words starts with the tenth letter of the alphabet and ends with the eighteenth?

    JIGSAW   KITTEN   KETTLES   JUNIOR **1**

20 If the letters of ASSESSMENT were put in alphabetical order, which letter would come seventh? **1**

If these words were written backwards and then placed in alphabetical order, which word would come fifth? Underline your answer.

21 slowly	happily	softly	friendly	normally
22 glanced	misplaced	polished	showed	charged
23 blacksmith	fifth	health	truth	warmth
24 vitamin	javelin	entertain	satin	captain
25 parent	absent	accident	confront	vacant

Total **25**

Mixed Papers

Mixed Paper 1

Synonyms

3 mins

Find a word that is similar in meaning to the word in capital letters and that rhymes with the second word.

Example   CABLE   tyre   *wire*

1	ELECTRICITY	tower	....	1
2	SHORELINE	toast	....	1
3	A LOT OF CATTLE	word	....	1
4	PART OF A SHIRT	dollar	....	1
5	TIMEPIECE	mock	....	1

Finding Words and Letters

3 mins

Rearrange the muddled letters in capitals to make a proper word. The answer will complete the sentence sensibly.

Example   A BEZAR is an animal with stripes.   *ZEBRA*

6	We spread TTREBU on bread.	....	1
7	Children often have BYRUGB knees!	....	1
8	The African LPHEEANT has big ears.	....	1

9 Put your TRELTI in the bin! .... `1`

10 We put letters in NVEEESLOP. .... `1`

⏱ 5 mins

Find the three-letter word which can be added to the letters in capitals to make a new word. The new word will complete the sentence sensibly.

Example The cat sprang onto the MO. **USE**

11 Please wash your HS before lunch. .... `1`

12 The DPING tap kept me awake. .... `1`

13 She is very NY and makes us laugh a lot. .... `1`

14 It was much DER now that the lights had been turned off. .... `1`

15 His HING was poor: he couldn't hear people talking. .... `1`

⏱ 3 mins

Remove one letter from the word in capital letters to leave a new word. The meaning of the new word is given in the clue.

Example AUNT an insect **ant**

16 BEAT a flying mammal .... `1`

17 COAST the price of something .... `1`

18 FEVER   always   1

19 PLANE   window glass   1

20 SLING   to make a musical sound using a voice   1

⏱ 3 mins

Write the four-letter word hidden at the end of one word and the beginning of the next word. The order of the letters may not be changed.

Example   The children had bat**s and** balls.   sand

21 Not only is the stamp attractive but it is also valuable.   1

22 It was the tallest tower ever seen.   1

23 My poor mother had four operations.   1

24 Izzy's rabbit chewed a hole in her hutch.   1

25 Well done, you're the last one out.   1

Word Progressions

⏱ 3 mins

Move one letter from the first word and add it to the second word to make two new words.

Example   hunt   sip   hut snip

26 bear   link   1

27 plan   fit   1

28	land	fake	....	....		1	
29	done	well	....	....		1	
30	stun	peal	....	....		1	

Sorting Words and Letters

3 mins

Complete the following sentences by selecting the most sensible word from each group of words given in the brackets. Underline the words selected.

Example The (children, books, foxes) carried the (houses, books, steps) home from the (greengrocer, library, factory).

31 Tim wears a black (shirt, handkerchief, scarf) when he plays (whist, football, scrabble) for the school (journey, team, work).

32 My pencil (grater, sharpener, cutter) is in my (cup, bed, bag) hanging on my (tree, floor, chair).

33 The (car, plane, ship) went into the (house, harbour, shed) very (slowly, cleverly, badly).

34 He (listened, watched, thought) very hard to (hear, catch, throw) the train (floating, going, coming) towards him.

35 In the (Sahara, Antarctic, jungle) icebergs are as (small, old, huge) as (penguins, garages, houses).

Substitution, Number and Logic

4 mins

Find the missing number by using the two numbers outside the brackets in the same way as the other sets of numbers.

Example   2 [8] 4   3 [18] 6   5 [**25**] 5

36 11 [23] 12   6 [15] 9   18 [__] 11   1

37 6 [19] 25   7 [10] 17   9 [__] 23   1

38 7 [2] 14   11 [3] 33   6 [__] 6   1

39 3 [30] 5   7 [42] 3   6 [__] 2   1

40 8 [24] 3   6 [30] 5   9 [__] 8   1

5 mins

Fill in the crosswords so that all the given words are included. You have been given one letter as a clue in each crossword.

41

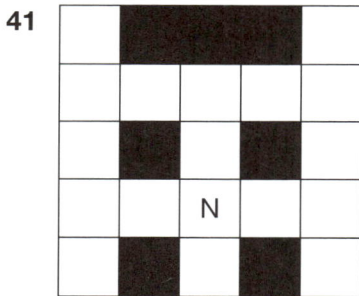

stiff, none, meter, tense, fence

42

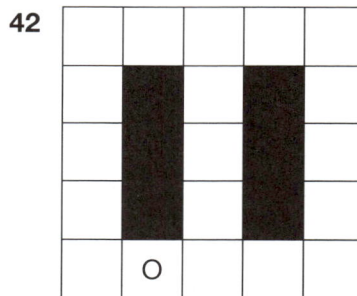

timer, torch, reach, treat, motor   2

43

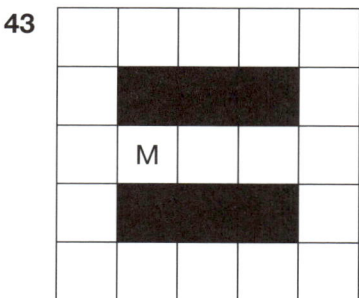

amble, horse, erect, heaps, sport

44

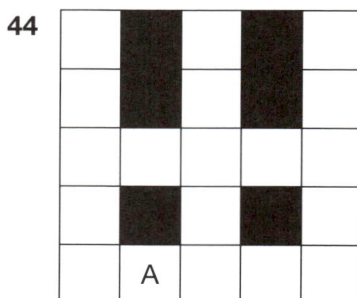

funny, layer, laser, towel, wands   2

Sorting Words and Letters

Rearrange the letters in capitals to make another word. The new word has something to do with the first two words.

Example   spot   soil   SAINT   STAIN

45	rock	pebble	NOTES	....	1
46	challenge	attempt	DEAR	....	1
47	bush	plant	BRUSH	....	1
48	box	container	TRACE	....	1
49	end	back	RARE	....	1

Codes

50	If 2124 stands for PIPE, 214 stands for	....	1
51	If 2867 stands for LINK, 786 stands for	....	1
52	If 5234 stands for WEAR, 342 stands for	....	1
53	If 3216 stands for WRAP, 613 stands for	....	1
54	If 1729 stands for COAT, 219 stands for	....	1

Substitution, Number and Logic

8 mins

If these words were placed in alphabetical order, which word would come fourth?

55 lounge locket locals loaded lonely 1

56 marry blank every blown march 1

If these words were listed in reverse alphabetical order, which word would come second?

57 racket raisin raffle rattle rascal 1

58 splint spoken square superb spread 1

59 concert foreign collect purpose puppets 1

60 Six families live in South Street. From the information below, work out which family lives in which house and write them in on the chart.

Browns
....

| 1 | | 3 | | 5 |

SOUTH STREET

| 2 | | 4 | | 6 |

....

The Greys live between the Blacks and the Whites on the even side on South Street.

The Greens live opposite the Blacks.

The Browns live in Number 1.

The Blues live in a house with a higher number than the Whites.

5

Total 64

Mixed Paper 2

Synonyms

Underline the two words, one from each group, which are closest in meaning.

Example (race, shop, start) (finish, begin, end)

1 (choose, time, bend) (trick, open, curve) | 1 |

2 (big, heavy, small) (old, slight, alike) | 1 |

3 (create, ruin, ignore) (invite, call, destroy) | 1 |

4 (author, book, story) (easel, painter, writer) | 1 |

5 (run, travel, fast) (slow, carry, swift) | 1 |

Finding Words and Letters

Find the three-letter word which can be added to the letters in capitals to make a new word. The new word will complete the sentence sensibly.

Example The cat sprang onto the MO. USE

6 We plant CABES in our vegetable garden each year. .... | 1 |

7 The HST boy returned the wallet he found on the road. .... | 1 |

8 'Take out some PR and a pencil,' said the teacher. .... | 1 |

9 I like to have lettuce and TOOES in my salad. .... | 1 |

10 My mum makes me hot tea with lemon when I have a sore THR. .... | 1 |

Sorting Words and Letters

Underline the one word which can be made from the letters of the word in capitals.

Example   CHAMPION   camping   notch   peach   cramp   <u>chimp</u>

11	HEAVE	head	have	vast	hive	hovel
12	BROTHER	another	there	broke	throb	bribe
13	FORCE	care	forge	core	fudge	free
14	GROPE	grape	rope	grip	rogue	pear
15	HANDS	shape	shore	ship	shade	sand

3 mins

Finding Words and Letter

Write the four-letter word hidden at the end of one word and the beginning of the next word. The order of the letters may not be changed.

Example   The children had bat<u>s and</u> balls.   sand

16   I don't like the clothes in this shop.   ....

17   The cinema shows new films each week.   ....

18   Running around helps tire you out.   ....

19   There's been an accident; come at once!   ....

20   Jade received letters from people she had never heard of.   ....

3 mins

Word Progressions

3 mins

Move one letter from the first word and add it to the second word to make two new words.

Example   hunt   sip   hut   snip

21 fear   can   1

22 spoil   eat   1

23 hoist   pant   1

24 haunt   lid   1

25 drear   spot   1

Sorting Words and Letters

6 mins

Complete the following sentences by selecting the most sensible word from each group of words given in the brackets. Underline the words selected.

Example   The (children, books, foxes) carried the (houses, books, steps) home from the (greengrocer, library, factory).

26 Jane has to go to the (house, cinema, school) as she has an (silly, important, small)

exam and she (fears, hopes, wonders) if she will do well.   1

27 Luckily she (ate, found, read) her (umbrella, book, lunch) just before the

(day, rain, bus) began.   1

28 In the event of a (silence, fire, flood) leave the (street, car, building) (slowly, badly, quickly).   1

29 I have lost my (ball, book, cat). She is (lazy, black, green) and has a (mouse, paw, collar).   1

30 He (ate, lost, drank) the lemonade quickly, (put on, took off, bought) his coat and

(swam, ran, left).   1

Find and underline the two words which need to change places for the sentence to make sense.

Example   She went to <u>letter</u> the <u>write</u>.

31 The better is weather now.   1

32 I'm supper forward to looking.   1

33 I like me book you gave the.   1

34 Up try to clean it do.   1

35 I vase over the knocked.   1

Sequences

3 mins

Fill in the missing letters and numbers.

Example   AB is to CD as PQ is to **RS**).

36 A82 is to B81 as C80 is to _____ .   1

37 D19 is to E19 as F20 is to _____ .   1

38 C9 is to D12 as E15 is to _____ .   1

39 AB5 is to CD6 as EF7 is to _____ .   1

40 KLM is to MNO as OPQ is to _____ .   1

Antonyms

Underline the two words, one from each group, which are most opposite in meaning.

Example   (dawn, <u>early</u>, wake)   (<u>late</u>, stop, sunrise)

41   (still, quiet, sudden)   (motionless, active, silence)   1

42   (icy, freezing, warm)   (cool, cold, frosty)   1

43   (bend, loosen, crack)   (straighten, drop, catch)   1

44   (fix, trade, sell)   (destroy, repair, improve)   1

45   (inside, low, between)   (under, high, below)   1

Substitution, Number and Logic

Write these words backwards and put them in alphabetical order.

GAMBIT   GARLAND   GALLOP   GAMBLE   GATHER

_____   _____   _____   _____   _____

46   Which is now the first word?   1

47   Which is now the middle word?   1

48   Which two letters are in all the words?   1

49   When the word is written forwards, which word
     has all the letters after the first in alphabetical order?   1

50   What is the total number of As in the words?   1

Codes

If the code for **DETAINS** is **ghbjklm**, what are the codes for the following words?

51 NEAT .... `1` ☐

52 DENT .... `1` ☐

What do these codes stand for?

53 ghjl .... `1` ☐

54 mbjkl .... `1` ☐

Sorting Words and Letters

Choose the word or phrase that makes the sentence true.

Example A LIBRARY always has (posters, a carpet, <u>books</u>, DVDs, stairs).

55 A PARTY always has (cake, music, gifts, guests, games). `1` ☐

56 A DOG always has a (lead, collar, kennel, tag, coat). `1` ☐

57 A RESTAURANT always has (food, a patio, music, tablecloths, candles). `1` ☐

58 A CAR always has (passengers, air conditioning, a radio, a clock, a steering wheel). `1` ☐

59 A BOARD GAME always has (dice, rules, cards, a timer, a scorecard). `1` ☐

Sequences

Choose two words, one from each set of brackets, to complete the sentence in the best way.

Example   Tall is to (tree, <u>short</u>, colour) as narrow is to (thin, white, <u>wide</u>).

60 Combine is to (leave, destroy, add) as subtract is to (cover, move, reduce).   ☐ 1

61 Fail is to (lose, try, play) as draw is to (tie, improve, succeed).   ☐ 1

62 Trap is to (catch, deliver, ignore) as release is to (free, lose, protect).   ☐ 1

63 Donate is to (charge, win, give) as receive is to (accept, present, sell).   ☐ 1

64 Order is to (choose, command, use) as ask is to (answer, request, refuse).   ☐ 1

65 Erase is to (delete, highlight, insert) as ring is to (circle, finger, hoop).   ☐ 1

Total 65 ☐

Mixed Paper 3

Antonyms

⏱ 3 mins

Underline the two words which are the odd ones out in the following groups of words.

Example   black   <u>king</u>   purple   green   <u>house</u>

1	skip	lead	walk	run	iron
2	river	mountain	ocean	sea	hill
3	cross	kind	generous	angry	loving
4	red	sun	blue	moon	green
5	sunny	rest	warm	sleep	fine

1
1
1
1
1

Finding Words and Letters

⏱ 3 mins

Find the three-letter word which can be added to the letters in capitals to make a new word. The new word will complete the sentence sensibly.

Example   The cat sprang onto the MO.   <u>USE</u>

6   It was so cold it was SING.   1

7   The king shouted for his SERT.   1

8   He woke LY that morning.   1

9   She picked some PROSES in the wood.   1

10   The dog gave him a nasty SCCH.   1

Sorting Words and Letters

Underline two words, one from each group, that go together to form a new word. The word in the first group always comes first.

Example   (hand, <u>green</u>, for)   (light, <u>house</u>, sure)

11 (red, green, blue)   (fingers, bell, rose)   1

12 (sun, light, bright)   (rub, off, shine)   1

13 (short, tall, foot)   (step, sure, arm)   1

14 (now, after, before)   (wards, went, down)   1

15 (short, foot, hurt)   (good, goal, ball)   1

Mixed Paper 3

Finding Words and Letters

Write the four-letter word hidden at the end of one word and the beginning of the next word. The order of the letters may not be changed.

Example   The children had bat<u>s and</u> balls.   *sand*

16 My mother makes us keep our house tidy.   1

17 I like juice made from tropical fruits.   1

18 Each apple costs forty-nine pence.   1

19 After all those years, I was still interested in it.   1

20 Despite losing I don't regret changing   1

Word Progressions

Move one letter from the first word and add it to the second word to make two new words.

Example   hunt   sip   hut   snip

21	steam	key	....	....
22	float	her	....	....
23	stall	kin	....	....
24	bread	foe	....	....
25	print	ate	....	....

1
1
1
1
1

Sorting Words and Letters

Complete the following sentences by selecting the most sensible word from each group of words given in the brackets. Underline the words selected.

Example   The (children, books, foxes) carried the (houses, books, steps) home from the (greengrocer, library, factory).

26 She (tried, worked, walked) to get her (son, dog, daughter) to do his (radio, drink, homework).

27 The (number, letter, sign) at the end of the (road, word, sum) says (come, run, stop).

28 The (ship, plane, car) in the (lane, sea, sky) is (driving, flying, sailing) very high.

29 We (swam, walked, skipped) as (slowly, lazily, quickly) as we could to get to the (castle, cloud, friend) before dark.

30 The (police, villagers, highwaymen) stopped the (canoe, cart, coach) and stole the travellers' (food, shoes, gold).

1
1
1
1
1

Sequences

3 mins

Fill in the missing letters.

31 AC is to EG as JL is to _____. [1]

32 AB is to WX as CD is to ____. [1]

33 ACE is to BDF as LNP is to ___. [1]

34 AZ is to BY as CX is to ___. [1]

35 ACB is to BCA as EGF is to ___. [1]

Substitution, Number and Logic

4 mins

Fill in the crosswords so that all the given words are included. You have been given one letter as a clue in each crossword.

36

	■		■	
	N			
	■		■	

anvil, orbit, brave, tails, organ

37

	■		■	
			R	
	■		■	
	■		■	

ochre, least, chest, ports, tusks [2]

38

			D	
	■	■		
	■	■		

caged, dares, cheer, ropes, elder

39

■		■		
			S	
■		■		

punch, sighs, husks, sates, night [2]

Sorting Words and Letters

Change one word so that the sentence makes sense. Underline the word you are taking out and write your new word on the line.

Example I waited in line to buy a <u>book</u> to see the film. *ticket*

40 If you don't eat fish or fruit you are a vegetarian. .... `1`

41 In a car you should always draw a seat belt. .... `1`

42 In Chinese restaurants many people read with chopsticks. .... `1`

43 Noughts and stars is a fun game to play with friends. .... `1`

44 It was so hot last night that a tree in our garden was blown over. .... `1`

Codes

Here are the number codes for four words. Match the right word to the right code.

SHOE	SOW	ROSE	WHOSE	SHOW
5 7 6 2	5 7 6 1	2 7 6 5 1	8 6 5 1	5 6 2

45 SHOE .... `1`

46 WHOSE .... `1`

47 SOW .... `1`

48 SHOW .... `1`

49 ROSE .... `1`

Sequences

Choose two words, one from each set of brackets, to complete the sentences in the best way.

Example   Tall is to (tree, <u>short</u>, colour) as narrow is to (thin, white, <u>wide</u>).

50   Dusk is to (evening, dark, moon) as dawn is to (sunset, night, morning).

51   Common is to (few, ordinary, lost) as unique is to (unusual, broken, expensive).

52   Sudden is to (skilled, quiet, swift) as gradual is to (steady, new, careless).

53   Leaning is to (tilted, standing, thin) as upright is to (vertical, fallen, lying).

54   Horse is to (ride, saddle, hoof) as dog is to (bone, walk, pet).

Substitution, Number and Logic

If a = 2, b = 3, c = 4, d = 5, find the answer to the following calculations.

55   a + b + c = ...

56   (c + d) ÷ b = ...

Finding Words and Letters

Find the letter which will complete both pairs of words, ending the first word and starting the second. The same letter must be used for both pairs of words.

Example mea (**t**) able   fi (**t**) ub

57 man (_) awn   da (_) et   **1**

58 tra (_) ea   ho (_) it   **1**

59 daw (_) ote   mai (_) un   **1**

60 pas (_) aw   wa (_) ty   **1**

61 bea (_) ry   be (_) ew   **1**

Synonyms

Find a word that is similar in meaning to the word in capital letters and that rhymes with the second word.

Example CABLE   tyre   wire

62 A FISH   spout **1**

63 HOUSE   comb **1**

64 FOG   hissed **1**

Total **64**

Mixed Paper 4

Antonyms

1–5 Look at these groups of words.

A	B	C	D
mule	theatre	spanner	purple
monkey	town hall	anvil	pink

Choose the correct group for each of the words below. Write in the letter.

bridge [__]   drill [__]   ferret   [__]   baboon [__]

arcade [__]   rose [__]   cinema [__]   beige   [__]

mole   [__]   saw [__]

5

Underline the two words, one from each group, which are the most opposite in meaning.

Example   (dawn, <u>early</u>, wake)   (<u>late</u>, stop, sunrise)

6   (break, whole, part)   (mend, fast, heal)

1

7   (long, land, stretch)   (length, measure, shrink)

1

8   (heat, empty, weight)   (bottom, full, light)

1

9   (lost, frighten, plentiful)   (lots, scarce, scare)

1

10   (fight, top, winner)   (left, loser, first)

1

Finding Words and Letters

Find the letter which will end the first word and start the second word.

Example   peac (**h**) ome

11 num (__) read

12 pip (__) ver

13 tos (__) oak

14 pla (__) ell

15 tha (__) int

Sorting Words and Letters

Underline the one word which cannot be made from the letters of the word in capital letters.

Example   STATIONERY   stone   tyres   ration   <u>nation</u>   noisy

16	TERRACE	care	rate	stain	trace	crate
17	DISTANT	stead	stand	stint	ants	dint
18	PAINTER	trip	rain	tramp	nape	print
19	GENERAL	large	near	rage	gear	ages
20	CLEAREST	clean	real	star	race	steer

3 mins

3 mins

Finding Words and Letters

3 mins

Write the four-letter word hidden at the end of one word and the beginning of the next word. The order of the letters may not be changed.

Example   The children had bat<u>s and</u> balls.   sand

21 Going to the seaside is an ideal tonic.   1

22 The cup is beside a bunch of flowers.   1

23 Her teeth are white and beautifully clean.   1

24 It means it is easy to control.   1

25 We think that our ways are best.   1

Word Progressions

3 mins

Change the first word into the last word by changing one letter at a time and making a new, different word in the middle.

Example   CASE   CASH   LASH

26 GEAR   ....   HEAL   1

27 FIRM   ....   HARM   1

28 BULB   ....   SULK   1

29 WISE   ....   WANE   1

30 SEAT   ....   SEND   1

Sorting Words and Letters

Complete the following sentences by selecting the most sensible word from each group of words given in the brackets. Underline the words selected.

Example   The (<u>children</u>, books, foxes) carried the (houses, <u>books</u>, steps) home from the (greengrocer, <u>library</u>, factory).

31 The day was (frosty, sunny, raining) and the (dog, woman, baby) went to sunbathe at the (town, slopes, beach).

1 ☐

32 It was (spring, summer, autumn), the trees were (brown, dead, green) and the (toads, birds, lambs) were in the fields.

1 ☐

33 We ran (yesterday, tomorrow, quickly) to the (house, shop, station) as we didn't want to miss the (truck, bike, train).

1 ☐

34 The (wheelbarrow, boat, tree) hit the (rock, grass, rain) so hard that (water, ice, birds) came on board.

1 ☐

35 We (ran, walked, jumped) overboard. The water was (dirty, muddy, cold) but we warmed up as we (drank, swam, ate).

1 ☐

Synonyms

Underline the one word in the brackets which will go equally well with both the pairs of words outside the brackets.

Example   rush, attack cost, fee   (price, hasten, strike, <u>charge</u>, money)

36 untruth, false   rest, lounge   (sleep, invent, fall, lie, support)   1

37 group, gang   fill, box   (tie, luggage, pack, carry, crate)   1

38 planet, sun   performer, celebrity   (moon, sky, actor, hero, star)   1

39 considerate, nice   type, sort   (gentle, kind, set, class, friendly)   1

40 cool, chilly   flu, infection   (freezing, sneeze, illness, cold, icy)   1

Substitution, Number and Logic

4 mins

Fill in the crosswords so that all the given words are included. You have been given one letter as a clue in each crossword.

41

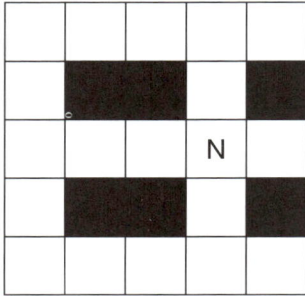

paper, paint, react,
tonic, party

42

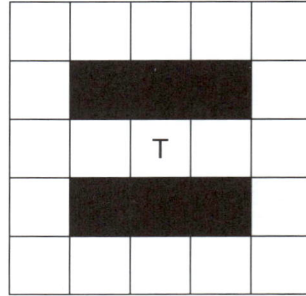

holds, patio, onset,
hippo, shout

2

43

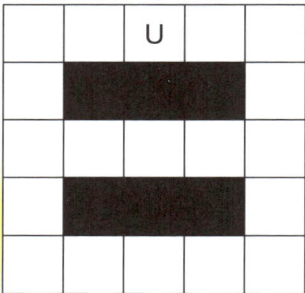

knots, pluck, hoops,
perch, radio

44

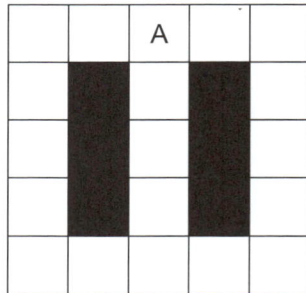

craze, error, after,
rarer, clear

2

Sequences

⏱ 3 mins

Give the two missing groups of letters and numbers in the following sequences.

The alphabet has been written out to help you.

A B C D E F G H I J K L M N O P Q R S T U V W X Y Z

| **Example** | CQ | DP | EQ | FP | **GQ** | **HP** |

45 ____ EQ FR DS ET ____ [1]

46 128J 64L 32N 16P ____ ____ [1]

47 AA BA ____ DB EC ____ [1]

48 8C 5B ____ ____ 8Y 5X [1]

49 ____ ____ DW CX BY AZ [1]

Codes

⏱ 3 mins

If the code for **GRATE** is △○◆❞① , what are the codes for the following words?

50 RATE .... [1]

51 EAR .... [1]

What do these codes stand for?

52 ❞◆△ .... [1]

53 ❞①◆ .... [1]

54 △○①◆❞ .... [1]

Sequences

3 mins

The first 10 letters of the alphabet are written as the first 10 numbers, i.e. A = 1, B = 2 etc.

Write these as numbers.

55 HIDE .... `1`

56 CAGED .... `1`

What are these words?

57 61354 .... `1`

58 854754 .... `1`

59 25138 ....

Substitution, Number and Logic

3 mins

Underline the word in each line that has its letters in alphabetical order.

60 word   act   letter   seen   frog   `1`

61 omelette   gasp   belt   through   under   `1`

62 know   gain   team   soon   from   `1`

63 spoon   pram   night   brag   moor   `1`

64 slice   peach   dunk   sty   frail   `1`

Total 64

Curveball Questions 2

Unusual and More Challenging Sequences

Sometimes with Verbal Reasoning you have to think outside the box.

1   If you reach the end of the alphabet, continue on to the next: X Y Z A B C. Think of it as less of an alphabet line – more of a circle going round continuously backwards as well as forwards.

2   If numbers are going up and down, ask yourself, could this be an alternating pattern, like this:

$$2 \quad 12 \quad 4 \quad 9 \quad 6 \quad 6 \quad 8 \quad 3 \quad \underline{\quad} \quad \underline{\quad}$$

Look at alternate numbers:

$$\mathbf{2} \quad 12 \quad \mathbf{4} \quad 9 \quad \mathbf{6} \quad 6 \quad \mathbf{8} \quad 3 \quad \mathbf{10} \quad \mathbf{0}$$

The first, third, fifth and seventh numbers are going up in twos.

The second, fourth, sixth and eighth numbers are going down in threes.

3   In number and letter sequences, you can get a repeating pattern where the same numbers/ letters are repeated.

With some number sequences, you can get questions that expect you to add one, then add two, then add three, for example, like this:

$$6 \quad 7 \quad 9 \quad 12 \quad 16 \quad 21 \quad \mathbf{27} \quad \mathbf{35}$$
$$+1 \quad +2 \quad +3 \quad +4 \quad +5 \quad +6 \quad +7 \quad +8$$

Or doubling/halving:

$$2 \quad 4 \quad 8 \quad 16 \quad \text{or} \quad 100 \quad 50 \quad 25 \quad 12\tfrac{1}{2}$$

or alternating, say, +2, +5, +2, +5, +2, +5.

20 mins

1	___	ZR	YT	XV	WX	VZ	___			1	
2	ZK	___	BQ	CT	___	EZ	FC			1	
3	3Z8	___	5V6	___	7R4	8P3	9N2			1	
4	A3	A4	___	B9	___	C18	D24			1	
5	7	15	9	17	___	___	13			1	
6	BB	___	DH	___	FN	GQ				1	
7	___	UB	XC	SD	VE	___				1	
8	FS	IQ	HO	___	JK	___				1	
9	___	___	JK	NO	RS	VW				1	
10	QR	___	YN	___	GJ	KH				1	
11	OR	SV	WZ	___	___	IL				1	
12	___	EX	GZ	___	KD	MF				1	
13	111	106	101	___	___	86				1	
14	81	___	63	___	45	36				1	
15	5	10	14	___	___	20				1	
16	666	66.6	___	___	0.0666					1	
17	6	___	12	20	___	24	24	28		1	
18	___	6	___	24	48	96				1	

#								
19	55	50	51	___	___	42	43	38
20	7	12	11	17	___	23	22	___
21	8	13	___	16	14	___	17	22
22	7	17	11	21	16	25	___	___
23	___	9	16	25	___	49	64	81
24	5	7	11	___	___	19	23	25
25	8	___	2	1	___	$\frac{1}{4}$		

1
1
1
1
1
1
1

Total
25

Unusual and More Challenging Sequences

Test Paper 1

Test Paper 1

60 mins

Underline the pair of words most similar in meaning.

Example   come, go   <u>roam, wander</u>   fear, fare

1   appreciation, thanks   please, prize   gale, calm   `1` ☐

2   present, past   paper, bins   creak, squeak `1` ☐

3   unknown, famous   gallant, brave   soap, brush   `1` ☐

4   rubbish, litter   noun, verb   noisy, quiet   `1` ☐

5   hour, time   silence, quietness   dust, polish   `1` ☐

Find the letter which will end the first word and start the second word.

Example   peac (**h**) ome

6   whe (__) ettle   `1` ☐

7   fea (__) ubber   `1` ☐

8   swor (__) elight `1` ☐

9   ste (__) ount   `1` ☐

10 soun (__) awn   `1` ☐

Underline one word in the brackets which is most opposite in meaning to the word in capitals.

Example   WIDE   (broad   vague   long   <u>narrow</u>   motorway)

11 ODD   (peculiar   queer   strange   even   unjust)   `1`

12 SHALLOW   (deep   water   dive   puddle   shape)   `1`

13 WHOLE   (complete   part   some   never   here)   `1`

14 SAD   (miserable   joyful   sorry   hopeless   hateful)   `1`

15 START   (begin   open   commence   end   first)   `1`

Look at the first group of three words. The word in the middle has been made from the other two words. Complete the second group of three words in the same way, making a new word in the middle.

Example   PAIN   INTO   TOOK   ALSO   <u>SOON</u>   ONLY

16 COMB BALE ALES   PART . . . .   RAPS   `1`

17 WIDE DESK SKIP   SITE . . . .   AMPS   `1`

18 OPEN NOSE SENT   RAID . . . .   AGUE   `1`

19 SAGE GETS TEST   MAST . . . .   TONE   `1`

20 FREE REEL SEAL   SPOT . . . .   FRET   `1`

Underline two words, one from each group, that go together to form a new word. The word in the first group always comes first.

Example   (hand, <u>green</u>, for)   (light, <u>house</u>, sure)

21 (no, two, duet)   (end, here, thing)   `1`

22 (drive, steer, car)   (hat, road, pet)   `1`

23 (land, earth, sky)   (mark, road, way)   `1`

24 (how, an, why)   (self, other, is)   `1`

25 (cot, bed, sleep)   (stead, stroll, stand)   `1`

Write the four-letter word hidden at the end of one word and the beginning of the next word. The order of the letters may not be changed.

Example   The children had bat<u>s and</u> balls.   **sand**

26 A single apple is very good for you.   `1`

27 This kind of behaviour is useless.   `1`

28 To speak like that isn't allowed.   `1`

29 You will need to write that far more neatly.   `1`

30 Come quickly or you will be too late.   `1`

Change the first word into the last word by changing one letter at a time and making a new, different word in the middle.

Example   CASE   CASH   LASH

31 FAKE   . . . .   BALE

32 LARK   . . . .   MARE

33 MADE   . . . .   CAKE

34 SONG   . . . .   LONE

35 COLD   . . . .   COOT

Find and underline the two words which need to change places for the sentence to make sense.

Example   She went to <u>letter</u> the <u>write</u>.

36 Do borrow want to you it?

37 Where shoes your are?

38 I must one a new buy.

39 It clean I'll tomorrow.

40 I full I'll get hope marks.

Test Paper 1

Choose two words, one from each set of brackets, to complete the sentence in the best way.

Example   Smile is to happiness as (drink, <u>tear</u>, shout) is to (whisper, laugh, <u>sorrow</u>).

41 Depart is to leave as (change, ignore, finish) is to (remain, begin, conclude). `1`

42 Heat is to warm as (wash, freeze, chop) is to (cool, boil, bake). `1`

43 Pence is to pound as (second, day, month) is to (minute, century, decade). `1`

44 Find is to lose as (easy, earth, ebb) is to (sun, flow, world). `1`

45 Midnight is to night as (evening, noon, night) is to (day, dawn, winter). `1`

Choose the word or phrase that makes the sentence true.

Example   A LIBRARY always has (posters, a carpet, <u>books</u>, DVDs, stairs).

46 A BANK always has (sweets, music, coffee, money, a guard). `1`

47 A CAMERA always has (film, a strap, a case, a lens, a stand). `1`

48 A PIANO always has (keys, music, a music stand, a seat, a clock). `1`

49 A CHAIR always has (wheels, arms, a cushion, a seat, a footrest). `1`

50 A FATHER always has a (cat, hobby, child, car, daughter). `1`

If the code for **AVERAGE** is ◆ ❞ ○ ① ◆ △ ○ , what are the codes for the following words?

51 VEER   . . . . `1`

52 REAR   . . . . `1`

What do these codes stand for?

53 △ ◯ ◆ ① ....

54 ◯ ◆ △ ◯ ① ....

55 △ ◆ ❞ ◯ ....

If A = 1, B = 2, C = 3, D = 4, E = 5, F = 6, find the sum of these words.

56 F + E + E + D = ...

57 C + A + F + E = ...

58 B + E + A + D = ...

59 F + A + C + E = ...

60 D + E + A + F = ...

Five children did a test for which 100 marks were awarded. R lost 4 marks, M had half as many marks as the person who came top, G lost 5 marks, D had 7 marks fewer than G and S had 12 marks fewer than R.

61 Who came top? ....

62 Who was 2nd? ....

63 Who came 3rd? ....

64 Who came 4th? ....

65 Who came 5th? ....

Read the first two statements and then underline two of the options below that must be true.

66–67 'My car is red; so are fire engines. My sister's car is a Ford. Ford make vans.'

All Ford cars are red.	I like Ford cars.
My car is a Ford.	Ford make fire engines.
I have a fire engine.	Ford make cars.
My sister's car is red.	Fire engines have a siren.
Fire engines are red.	My sister is a firefighter.

2

Rearrange the letters in capitals to make another word. The new word has something to do with the first two words.

Example spot soil SAINT **STAIN**

68 cut rip RATE **1**

69 pipe tube SHOE **1**

70 whiskers moustache BREAD **1**

Rearrange these words into a sentence that makes sense. Underline the word that you do not need.

Example walk school my minutes hour ten takes to

(My walk to school takes ten minutes.)

71 Eve tomorrow tree shouted it's children the Christmas **1**

72 the in allotment vegetables carrot amazing are our **1**

73 onto the crashed angrily storm beach waves the **1**

Which one letter can be added to the front of all of these words to make new words?

Example   <u>c</u>are   <u>c</u>at   <u>c</u>rate   <u>c</u>art   <u>c</u>one

74 __eat   __one   __ice   __ote   [1]

75 __ail   __ape   __ear   __here   [1]

76 __act   __lag   __all   __ace   [1]

77 __air   _all   __and   __old   [1]

Work out the missing synonym. Spell the new word correctly, putting one letter in each space.

Example   strange p e <u>c</u> u <u>l</u> i <u>a</u> r

78 giggle   c _ u c k __ e   [1]

79 uneven   i r r e __ u __ a r   [1]

80 finish   t e r __ i n a __ e   [1]

Total 80

Test Paper 2

60 mins

Change one word so that the sentence makes sense. Underline the word you are taking out and write your new word on the line.

Example   I waited in line to buy a <u>book</u> to see the film.   *ticket*

1   Summer is my favourite season because I love it when it snows. **1**

2   I sent out newspapers to everyone I wanted to come to my

birthday party. **1**

3   My mother sings out a story to me before bed each night. **1**

4   The monkey is known as the king of the jungle. **1**

5   Elm, oak and maple are all types of flower. **1**

Underline the pair of words most opposite in meaning.

Example   cup, mug   coffee, milk   <u>hot, cold</u>

6   conceal, hide   front, back   modern, new   **1**

7   rough, smooth   rapid, quick   hope, help   **1**

8   tested, tried   bent, straight   gap, hole   **1**

9   stern, strict   ally, friend   sell, buy   **1**

10 here, there   show, display   angry, cross   **1**

Remove two letters from the word in capital letters to leave a new word. The meaning of the new word is given in the clue.

Example   MONKEY   lives in a monastery   _monk_

11	HOUSES	tube	. . . .	1
12	GRAPES	knocks	. . . .	1
13	SWARMS	not cool	. . . .	1
14	THINGS	not that	. . . .	1
15	SHEATH	chair	. . . .	1

Find a word that can be put in front of each of the following words to make new words.

Example   cast   fall   ward   pour   _down_

16	bow	drop	fall	coat	. . . .	1
17	guard	fly	work	place	. . . .	1
18	ache	brush	paste	pick	. . . .	1
19	show	works	block	worthy	. . . .	1
20	struck	beam	light	stone	. . . .	1

Write the four-letter word hidden at the end of one word and the beginning of the next word. The order of the letters may not be changed.

Example   The children had bats <u>and</u> balls.   _sand_

21	For his birthday, I got Dad new socks.	. . . .	1
22	The next time he snaps, I'm going!	. . . .	1

23 The art teacher was unwell today. . . . . `1`

24 She missed her turn due to long queues. . . . . `1`

25 Areas of path on the cliff under our feet were slippery. . . . . `1`

Look at the first group of three words. The word in the middle has been made from the other two words. Complete the second group of three words in the same way, making a new word in the middle of the group.

Example   PAIN   INTO   TOOK   ALSO   <u>SOON</u>   ONLY

26 CODE   COST   FAST   FROG   . . . .   GLEE `1`

27 DECK   KICK   SICK   KIND   . . . .   LEAD `1`

28 OPEN   PETS   POTS   DISK   . . . .   ABLE `1`

29 CLAP   PLAN   NAPE   CRAB   . . . .   TASK `1`

30 SLIP   PILL   LOUD   DRAB   . . . .   KNOW `1`

Find and underline the two words which need to change places for the sentence to make sense.

Example   She went to <u>letter</u> the <u>write</u>.

31 Do Street live on the High you? `1`

32 It is wilting and the flowers are hot. `1`

33 I've paper all the used already. `1`

34 The blissfully slept cat in the sun. `1`

35 I feel in sick a car. `1`

Underline the word in the brackets closest in meaning to the word in capitals.

Example UNHAPPY (unkind death laughter <u>sad</u> friendly)

36 REPLY (question comment answer write explain) `1`

37 DISCOVER (lose hide lock borrow find) `1`

38 EXAMINE (own paint fix study trick) `1`

39 TRUST (win believe pay stop consider) `1`

40 LONG (short small lengthy light thin) `1`

Fill in the crosswords so that all the given words are included. You have been given one letter as a clue in each crossword.

41

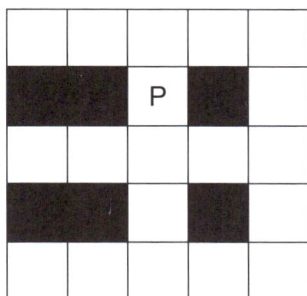

apple, super, years, syrup, bleep

42

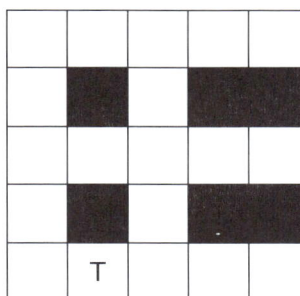

lemon, other, sense, lasso, munch `2`

43

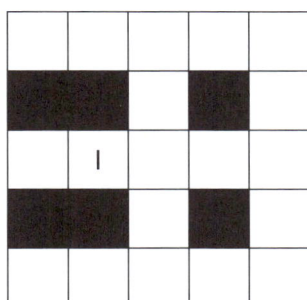

eager, night, shell, three, lathe

44

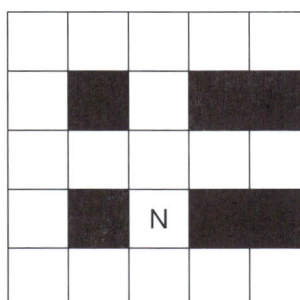

break, opens, score, sable, easel `2`

45

	■		■	
	■	H	■	
	■		■	

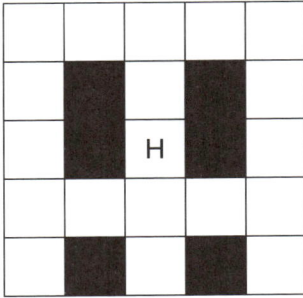

drear, arena, crowd, other, clear

In each line underline the word which would come in the middle if the words were arranged in alphabetical order.

46 RECKON   REASON   REBEL   READY   REALISE

47 SCHEME   SAILOR   SCENE   SCARED   SAFETY

48 DEPRESS   DELETE   DEPEND   DELIGHT   DELIVER

49 CLOSE   CHASE   CLIFF   CHAOS   CHART

50 BOILING   BRAWL   BLANK   BOAST   BLARE

Here are the codes for five words. Match the right word to the right code.

CHART	CHEAP	PEAR	PART	REACH
△430	△307	0431◆	1◆43△	1◆307

51 CHART   . . . .

52 CHEAP   . . . .

53 PEAR   . . . .

54 PART   . . . .

55 REACH   . . . .

Find the letter which will complete both pairs of words, ending the first word and starting the second. The same letter must be used for both pairs of words.

Example   mea (**t**) able   fi (**t**) ub

56 drin (__) now   flic (__) ite   `1`

57 stu (__) un   fla (__) at   `1`

58 til (__) yes   slim (__) nds   `1`

59 wor (__) ose   pla (__) ewt   `1`

60 mea (__) ight   fil (__) ost   `1`

Add one letter to the word in capital letters to make a new word. The meaning of the new word is given in the clue.

Example   PLAN   simple   _plain_

61 ARE   not covered   . . . .   `1`

62 MAN   most important   . . . .   `1`

63 RAT   a float   . . . .   `1`

64 OVER   put on top of   . . . .   `1`

65 SORT   little   . . . .   `1`

Work out the missing synonym. Spell the new word correctly, putting one letter in each space.

Example   strange p e _c u l i a_ r

66 brave   v a l __ __ n t   `1`

67 freedom   l i __ e r __ y   `1`

68 proud   a r r o __ __ n t   `1`

Match the correct codes to the words and work out the missing one.

BOOM	OMEN	BOMB
9 F 3 &	x 9 F x	

69 BOOM .... `1`

70 OMEN .... `1`

71 BOMB .... `1`

72 Using the same code, decode **F 9 9 &** .... `1`

Rearrange these words into a sentence that makes sense. Underline the word that you do not need.

Example walk   school   my   minutes   <u>hour</u>   ten   takes   to

(My walk to school takes ten minutes.)

73 trees   is   by   plant   it   important   to `1`

74 in   children   should   more   outside   play `1`

75 sky   are   low   aircraft   noisy   very   flying `1`

76 will   what   where   wearing   you   tonight   be `1`

Find a word that can be put in front of each of the following words to make new, compound words.

Example   cast   fall   ward   pour   <u>down</u>

77 storm   ball   plough   man   .... `1`

78 out   book   cuff   shake   .... `1`

79 fall   proof   tight   colour   .... `1`

80 ground   line   stand   arm   .... `1`

Total **80**

92

Keywords

Some special words and symbols are used in this book. You will find them in bold the first time they appear. These words are explained here.

anagram	a word made by rearranging the letters of another word.
antonym	a word with an opposite meaning to another word, for example wet, dry.
compound word	two or more words put together to make a new word.
consonant(s)	a letter that is not a vowel.
context	the situation in which something happens and that helps you to understand it.
deduction	the process of using information you have in order to find the answer to a problem.
logic	using sensible argument and thought.
reasoning	the process of thinking about something in a logical way.
root word	the main part of a word to which prefixes and/or suffixes can be added.
statement	a sentence that is not a question or an exclamation.
substitution	to take the place of something or someone else.
synonym	a word with a similar meaning to another word, for example, smile, grin.
value	a number that shows the result of a calculation.
verb	an action word that shows doing, having or being.
verbal	concerned with words only.
vocabulary	the range of words that a person knows and uses.
vowel(s)	any of the letters a, e, i, o, u and sometimes y.

11+ Study Guide

Essentials

- Don't worry too much about the level that you start at. Beginning with an easier book can help your confidence.

- Make sure you have the right equipment – you will need your pencils, an eraser and a notebook.

- This book contains skills guidance and worked examples, but if you need more help with technique, the Bond Handbooks might also be useful to you.

Studying Effectively

1 Turn to the first topic and read the Key Skills box. You might want to read it a few times or with someone else to understand it properly or to underline key words.

2 Read the worked example a few times and make sure you understand it.

3 In your notebook, write down the topic heading and the worked example on a new page. This is for you to revise and remember. Once you have completed the final book, you will have a super-useful notebook that you can use in secondary school.

4 Now set a timer – a kitchen timer, a watch or phone with an alarm – for the timed section.

5 Work your way through the questions carefully. If you don't know the answer to something, draw a circle around the question number and take your best guess. This is important as you can find patterns if you make mistakes and it highlights where you need to consolidate.

6 Ask someone to mark the paper for you or mark it yourself and see where you made mistakes. Is there a common pattern? For every mistake, decide if it is not knowing the technique properly, not consolidating the technique enough or a loss of focus, and label this next to each question using T = technique, C = consolidation, F = focus.

7 Have another go at the questions you made errors in to understand what you did wrong. If it is a vocabulary problem, write down the word with its meaning / synonym / antonym at the back of your book so that you widen your vocabulary range.

Making Mistakes

Everyone makes mistakes and they are an important part of how we learn. The reason we practise before an exam is so that we can make those mistakes in a safe space rather than in the test itself and that way we can learn from them and make fewer mistakes when it really matters.

Remember that there is no such thing as a 'silly mistake'. You are not silly, and neither is your mistake. It is usually not understanding the technique, not consolidating the skill needed so that it is only partially remembered, or you have lost focus. Losing focus does not mean that you have done something bad; it just means that your attention was on something else. These tips can help:

Not Understanding the Technique:

• Go back to the learning section and reread the key skills box.

• Look at the worked example that you have in your notebook.

• Use the Bond Handbook for more support.

Not Consolidating Enough:

• It is amazing how much consolidation is needed by everyone so don't worry about doing lots of additional questions.

• Look at Bond online for some more questions to help you revise.

• Ask someone to test you on the technique.

Losing Focus:

• Make sure that you are not too tired, hungry, thirsty or distracted.

• Work out where you have made a mistake and break it down into sections. It might be that you focus on tricky division, but go too fast when it comes to addition. It might be that you read the comprehension extract, but you lost focus and misread it.

• Once you have identified the problem area, make sure that in new questions, you check yourself and focus carefully.

Common Problems

'I don't have time to study.'

Make sure that you have a timetable that is doable. If you have lots of activities that take up time, perhaps break your work up. The books all have timing sections so fit in smaller sections when you can. It's important to talk to your parent if you feel that you need more time for your 11+ work.

'I find it hard to complete my homework as I want to play instead.'

Motivation is difficult for most people. Don't completely stop all fun activities during the 11+ but get a balance. Key to this is a timetable so you know when, what and where to study. Make sure it is doable and build in something fun if you complete your homework for the day. Another tip is to write down your reasons for doing the 11+. It might be to keep your family happy, to get into a school that your friends are going to, or even that the school is convenient. Ask yourself how important each reason is. Can you commit to the reasons you have? If so, keep remembering the reason and what will happen if you don't commit. Perhaps talk to your family so that they know how you feel.

'My friend is using different books to me.'

The Bond 11+ system covers English/Verbal Reasoning and Maths/Non-verbal reasoning/spatial awareness. Bond has had many decades of success in 11+ material. Many tutors will only use Bond for their pupils, and they get an exceptionally high pass rate. It doesn't mean that Bond is the only 11+ provider, so don't worry that your friend is using different material. What is important is that you are fully prepared for your online exam, and you can have confidence in the Bond system.

'I'm scared of failing.'

It is natural to feel that. Remember that you cannot climb a mountain in one gigantic step. You need lots and lots of little steps to get to the top. The 11+ is like that. You can't sit down and learn everything straight away, but the little steps you take will lead you to the exam. Remember that every mistake can be identified and once you identify it, you may be able to understand it and solve the problem for next time. Mistakes are perfection in progress! If a selective school is the best learning environment for you, then you can work little and often through the books and then test papers leading up to the exam. If you find it too much and you are working at your full potential already, then maybe a school that is not selective will suit your learning better. There is no 'best school' and 'worst school' for everyone. It is the best school for an individual child. Do talk to someone about your feelings though as you need to feel supported.

'My friend has a tutor. Do I need one?'

Whether or not to have tutor depends on many different factors, including where your particular strengths and challenges lie, your own approach to learning, and whether the costs involved are feasible. The Bond system is rigorous and aims to support every child with a range of books and learning materials. The Bond Handbooks can do the job of a tutor and many tutors also use the Bond books and Handbooks with their pupils. Bond has been providing 11+ material since the 1960s, helping thousands of pupils to pass their 11+ exams without having a tutor.

'I don't want to do the 11+ exam.'

This is a conversation to have with your family, but the best advice might be to follow the 11+ books anyway. They will teach you skills, techniques and methods that will give you self-confidence regardless of the secondary school you attend. No knowledge is a waste, and you will be keeping your options open.

There is more information on the Bond website. Bond has a Parent's Guide to the 11+ and there is a range of supportive printed and online material. See online for further details. **www.bond11plus.co.uk**